Apache Flume: Distributed Log Collection for Hadoop

Stream data to Hadoop using Apache Flume

Steve Hoffman

BIRMINGHAM - MUMBAI

Apache Flume: Distributed Log Collection for Hadoop

First published: July 2013

Production Reference: 1090713

Published by Packt Publishing Ltd.
Livery Place
35 Livery Street
Birmingham B3 2PB, UK.

ISBN 978-1-78216-791-4

www.packtpub.com

Cover Image by Abhishek Pandey (abhishek.pandey1210@gmail.com)

Credits

Author
Steve Hoffman

Reviewers
Subash D'Souza
Stefan Will

Acquisition Editor
Kunal Parikh

Commissioning Editor
Sharvari Tawde

Technical Editors
Jalasha D'costa
Mausam Kothari

Project Coordinator
Sherin Padayatty

Proofreader
Aaron Nash

Indexer
Monica Ajmera Mehta

Graphics
Valentina D'silva
Abhinash Sahu

Production Coordinator
Kirtee Shingan

Cover Work
Kirtee Shingan

About the Author

Steve Hoffman has 30 years of software development experience and holds
a B.S. in computer engineering from the University of Illinois Urbana-Champaign
and a M.S. in computer science from the DePaul University. He is currently
a Principal Engineer at Orbitz Worldwide.

More information on Steve can be found at `http://bit.ly/bacoboy` or on
Twitter `@bacoboy`.

This is Steve's first book.

I'd like to dedicate this book to my loving wife Tracy. Her dedication
to perusing what you love is unmatched and it inspires me to follow
her excellent lead in all things.

I'd also like to thank Packt Publishing for the opportunity to write
this book and my reviewers and editors for their hard work in
making it a reality.

Finally, I want to wish a fond farewell to my brother Richard who
passed away recently. No book has enough pages to describe in
detail just how much we will all miss him. Good travels brother.

About the Reviewers

Subash D'Souza is a professional software developer with strong expertise in crunching big data using Hadoop/HBase with Hive/Pig. He has worked with Perl/PHP/Python, primarily for coding and MySQL/Oracle as the backend, for several years prior to moving into Hadoop fulltime. He has worked on scaling for load, code development, and optimization for speed. He also has experience optimizing SQL queries for database interactions. His specialties include Hadoop, HBase, Hive, Pig, Sqoop, Flume, Oozie, Scaling, Web Data Mining, PHP, Perl, Python, Oracle, SQL Server, and MySQL Replication/Clustering.

I would like to thank my wife, Theresa for her kind words of support and encouragement.

Stefan Will is a computer scientist with a degree in machine learning and pattern recognition from the University of Bonn. For over a decade has worked for several startup companies in Silicon Valley and Raleigh, North Carolina, in the area of search and analytics. Presently, he leads the development of the search backend and the Hadoop-based product analytics platform at Zendesk, the customer service software provider.

www.PacktPub.com

Support files, eBooks, discount offers and more

You might want to visit www.PacktPub.com for support files and downloads related to your book.

Did you know that Packt offers eBook versions of every book published, with PDF and ePub files available? You can upgrade to the eBook version at www.PacktPub.com and as a print book customer, you are entitled to a discount on the eBook copy. Get in touch with us at service@packtpub.com for more details.

At www.PacktPub.com, you can also read a collection of free technical articles, sign up for a range of free newsletters and receive exclusive discounts and offers on Packt books and eBooks.

http://PacktLib.PacktPub.com

Do you need instant solutions to your IT questions? PacktLib is Packt's online digital book library. Here, you can access, read and search across Packt's entire library of books.

Why Subscribe?

- Fully searchable across every book published by Packt
- Copy and paste, print and bookmark content
- On demand and accessible via web browser

Free Access for Packt account holders

If you have an account with Packt at www.PacktPub.com, you can use this to access PacktLib today and view nine entirely free books. Simply use your login credentials for immediate access.

Table of Contents

Preface

Hadoop is a great open source tool for sifting tons of unstructured data into something manageable, so that your business can gain better insight into your customers, needs. It is cheap (can be mostly free), scales horizontally as long as you have space and power in your data center, and can handle problems your traditional data warehouse would be crushed under. That said, a little known secret is that your Hadoop cluster requires you to feed it with data; otherwise, you just have a very expensive heat generator. You will quickly find, once you get past the "playing around" phase with Hadoop, that you will need a tool to automatically feed data into your cluster. In the past, you had to come up with a solution for this problem, but no more! Flume started as a project out of Cloudera when their integration engineers had to keep writing tools over and over again for their customers to import data automatically. Today the project lives with the Apache Foundation, is under active development, and boasts users who have been using it in their production environments for years.

In this book I hope to get you up and running quickly with an architectural overview of Flume and a quick start guide. After that we'll deep-dive into the details on many of the more useful Flume components, including the very important File Channel for persistence of in-flight data records and the HDFS Sink for buffering and writing data into **HDFS**, the **Hadoop Distributed File System**. Since Flume comes with a wide variety of modules, chances are that the only tool you'll need to get started is a text editor for the configuration file.

By the end of the book, you should know enough to build out a highly available, fault tolerant, streaming data pipeline feeding your Hadoop cluster.

What this book covers

Chapter 1, Overview and Architecture, introduces the reader to Flume and the problem space that it is trying to address (specifically with regard to Hadoop). An architectural overview is given of the various components to be covered in the later chapters.

Chapter 2, Flume Quick Start, serves to get you up and running quickly, including downloading Flume, creating a "Hello World" configuration, and running it.

Chapter 3, Channels, covers the two major channels most people will use and the configuration options available for each.

Chapter 4, Sinks and Sink Processors, goes into great detail on using the HDFS Flume output, including compression options and options for formatting the data. Failover options are also covered to create a more robust data pipeline.

Chapter 5, Sources and Channel Selectors, will introduce several of the Flume input mechanisms and their configuration options. Switching between different channels based on data content is covered, allowing for the creation of complex data flows.

Chapter 6, Interceptors, ETL, and Routing, explains how to transform data in flight as well as extract information from the payload to use with channel selectors to make routing decisions. Tiering Flume agents is covered using Avro serialization, as well as using the Flume command line as a standalone Avro client for testing and importing data manually.

Chapter 7, Monitoring Flume, discusses various options available to monitor Flume both internally and externally including Monit, Nagios, Ganglia, and custom hooks.

Chapter 8, There Is No Spoon – The Realities of Real-time Distributed Data Collection, is a collection of miscellaneous things to consider that are outside the scope of just configuring and using Flume.

What you need for this book

You'll need a computer with a Java Virtual Machine installed, since Flume is written in Java. If you don't have Java on your computer, you can download it from http://java.com/.

You will also need an Internet connection so you can download Flume to run the Quick Start example.

This book covers Apache Flume 1.3.0, including a few items back-ported into Cloudera's Flume CDH4 distribution.

Who this book is for

This book is for people responsible for implementing the automatic movement of data from various systems into a Hadoop cluster. If it is your job to load data into Hadoop on a regular basis, this book should help you code yourself out of manual monkey-work or from writing a custom tool you'll be supporting for as long as you work at your company.

Only basic Hadoop knowledge of HDFS is required. Some custom implementations are covered should your needs necessitate it. For this level of implementation, you will need to know how to program in Java.

Finally, you'll need your favorite text editor since most of this book covers how to configure various Flume components via the agent's text configuration file.

Conventions

In this book, you will find a number of styles of text that distinguish between different kinds of information. Here are some examples of these styles, and an explanation of their meaning.

Code words in text are shown as follows: "We can include other contexts through the use of the `include` directive."

A block of code is set as follows:

```
agent.sinks.k1.hdfs.path=/logs/apache/access
agent.sinks.k1.hdfs.filePrefix=access
agent.sinks.k1.hdfs.fileSuffix=.log
```

When we wish to draw your attention to a particular part of a code block, the relevant lines or items are set in bold:

```
agent.sources.s1.command=uptime
agent.sources.s1.restart=true
agent.sources.s1.restartThrottle=60000
```

Any command-line input or output is written as follows:

```
$ tar -zxf apache-flume-1.3.1.tar.gz
$ cd apache-flume-1.3.1
```

New terms and **important words** are shown in bold.

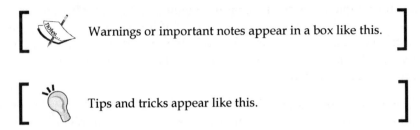

Warnings or important notes appear in a box like this.

Tips and tricks appear like this.

Reader feedback

Feedback from our readers is always welcome. Let us know what you think about this book—what you liked or may have disliked. Reader feedback is important for us to develop titles that you really get the most out of.

To send us general feedback, simply send an e-mail to feedback@packtpub.com, and mention the book title via the subject of your message. If there is a topic that you have expertise in and you are interested in either writing or contributing to a book, see our author guide on www.packtpub.com/authors.

Customer support

Now that you are the proud owner of a Packt book, we have a number of things to help you to get the most from your purchase.

Errata

Although we have taken every care to ensure the accuracy of our content, mistakes do happen. If you find a mistake in one of our books—maybe a mistake in the text or the code—we would be grateful if you would report this to us. By doing so, you can save other readers from frustration and help us improve subsequent versions of this book. If you find any errata, please report them by visiting http://www.packtpub.com/submit-errata, selecting your book, clicking on the **errata submission form** link, and entering the details of your errata. Once your errata are verified, your submission will be accepted and the errata will be uploaded on our website, or added to any list of existing errata, under the Errata section of that title. Any existing errata can be viewed by selecting your title from http://www.packtpub.com/support.

Piracy

Piracy of copyright material on the Internet is an ongoing problem across all media. At Packt, we take the protection of our copyright and licenses very seriously. If you come across any illegal copies of our works, in any form, on the Internet, please provide us with the location address or website name immediately so that we can pursue a remedy.

Please contact us at copyright@packtpub.com with a link to the suspected pirated material.

We appreciate your help in protecting our authors, and our ability to bring you valuable content.

Questions

You can contact us at questions@packtpub.com if you are having a problem with any aspect of the book, and we will do our best to address it.

1
Overview and Architecture

If you are reading this book, chances are you are swimming in mountains of data. Creating mountains of data has become very easy, thanks to Facebook, Twitter, Amazon, digital cameras and camera phones, YouTube, Google, and just about anything else you can think of connected to the Internet. As a provider of a website, 10 years ago, your application logs were only used to help you troubleshoot your website. Today, that same data can provide valuable insight into your business and customers if you know how to pan gold out of your river of data.

Furthermore, since you are reading this book, you are also aware that Hadoop was created to solve (partially) the problem of sifting through mountains of data. Of course, this only works if you can reliably load your Hadoop cluster with data for your data scientists to pick apart.

Getting data in and out of Hadoop (in this case, the **Hadoop File System (HDFS)**) isn't hard—it is just a simple command as follows:

```
% hadoop fs --put data.csv .
```

This works great when you have all your data neatly packaged and ready to upload.

But your website is creating data all the time. How often should you batch load data to HDFS? Daily? Hourly? Whatever processing period you choose, eventually somebody always asks, "can you get me the data sooner?" What you really need is a solution that can deal with streaming logs/data.

Turns out you aren't alone in this need. Cloudera, a provider of professional services for Hadoop as well as their own distribution of Hadoop, saw this need over and over while working with their customers. Flume was created to meet this need and create a standard, simple, robust, flexible, and extensible tool for data ingestion into Hadoop.

Flume 0.9

Flume was first introduced in Cloudera's CDH3 Distribution in 2011. It consisted of a federation of worker daemons (agents) configured from a centralized master (or masters) via Zookeeper (a federated configuration and coordination system). From the master you could check agent status in a Web UI, as well as push out configuration centrally from the UI or via a command line shell (both really communicating via Zookeeper to the worker agents).

Data could be sent in one of the three modes, namely, **best effort (BE)**, **disk failover (DFO)**, and **end-to-end (E2E)**. The masters were used for the end-to-end (E2E) mode acknowledgements and multi-master configuration never really matured so usually you had only one master making it a central point of failure for E2E data flows. Best effort is just what it sounds like—the agent would try and send the data, but if it couldn't, the data would be discarded. This mode is good for things like metrics where gaps can easily be tolerated, as new data is just a second away. Disk failover mode stores undeliverable data to the local disk (or sometimes a local database) and keeps retrying until the data can be delivered to the next recipient in your data flow. This is handy for those planned (or unplanned) outages as long as you have sufficient local disk space to buffer the load.

In June of 2011, Cloudera moved control of the Flume project to the Apache foundation. It came out of incubator status a year later in 2012. During that incubation year, work had already begun to refactor Flume under the Star Trek Themed tag, Flume-NG (Flume the Next Generation).

Flume 1.X (Flume-NG)

There were many reasons to why Flume was refactored. If you are interested in the details you can read about it at `https://issues.apache.org/jira/browse/` `FLUME-728`. What started as a refactoring branch eventually became the main line of development as Flume 1.X.

The most obvious change in Flume 1.X is that the centralized configuration master/masters and Zookeeper are gone. The configuration in Flume 0.9 was overly verbose and mistakes were easy to make. Furthermore, centralized configuration was really outside the scope of Flume's goals. Centralized configuration was replaced with a simple on-disk configuration file (although the configuration provider is pluggable so that it can be replaced). These configuration files are easily distributed using tools such as cf-engine, chef, and puppet. If you are using a Cloudera Distribution, take a look at Cloudera Manager to manage your configurations—their licensing was recently changed to lift the node limit so it may be an attractive option for you. Be sure you don't manage these configurations manually or you'll be editing those files manually forever.

Another major difference in Flume 1.X is that the reading of input data and the writing of output data are now handled by different worker threads (called Runners). In Flume 0.9, the input thread also did the writing to the output (except for failover retries). If the output writer was slow (rather than just failing outright), it would block Flume's ability to ingest data. This new asynchronous design leaves the input thread blissfully unaware of any downstream problem.

The version of Flume covered in this book is 1.3.1 (current at the time of this book's writing).

The problem with HDFS and streaming data/logs

HDFS isn't a real filesystem, at least not in the traditional sense, and many of the things we take for granted with normal filesystems don't apply here, for example being able to mount it. This makes getting your streaming data into Hadoop a little more complicated.

In a regular **Portable Operating System Interface (POSIX)** style filesystem, if you open a file and write data, it still exists on disk before the file is closed. That is, if another program opens the same file and starts reading, it will get the data already flushed by the writer to disk. Furthermore, if that writing process is interrupted, any portion that made it to disk is usable (it may be incomplete, but it exists).

In HDFS the file exists only as a directory entry, it shows as having zero length until the file is closed. This means if data is written to a file for an extended period without closing it, a network disconnect with the client will leave you with nothing but an empty file for all your efforts. This may lead you to the conclusion that it would be wise to write small files so you can close them as soon as possible.

The problem is Hadoop doesn't like lots of tiny files. Since the HDFS metadata is kept in memory on the NameNode, the more files you create, the more RAM you'll need to use. From a MapReduce prospective, tiny files lead to poor efficiency. Usually, each mapper is assigned a single block of a file as input (unless you have used certain compression codecs). If you have lots of tiny files, the cost of starting the worker processes can be disproportionally high compared to the data it is processing. This kind of block fragmentation also results in more mapper tasks increasing the overall job run times.

These factors need to be weighed when determining the rotation period to use when writing to HDFS. If the plan is to keep the data around for a short time, then you can lean towards the smaller file size. However, if you plan on keeping the data for very long time, you can either target larger files or do some periodic cleanup to compact smaller files into fewer larger files to make them more MapReduce friendly. After all, you only ingest the data once, but you might run a MapReduce job on that data hundreds or thousands of times.

Sources, channels, and sinks

The Flume agent's architecture can be viewed in this simple diagram. An input is called a **source** and an output is called a **sink**. A **channel** provides the glue between a **source** and a **sink**. All of these run inside a daemon called an **agent**.

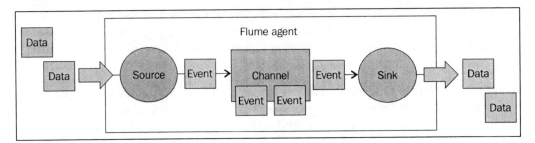

One should keep in mind the following things:

A **source** writes **events** to one or more **channels**.

A **channel** is the holding area as **events** are passed from a **source** to a **sink**.

A **sink** receives **events** from one **channel** only.

An **agent** can have many **sources, channels, and sinks**.

Flume events

The basic payload of data transported by Flume is called an event. An event is composed of zero or more headers and a body.

The headers are key/value pairs that can be used to make routing decisions or carry other structured information (such as the timestamp of the event or hostname of the server where the event originated). You can think of it as serving the same function as HTTP headers—a way to pass additional information that is distinct from the body.

The body is an array of bytes that contains the actual payload. If your input is comprised of tailed logfiles, the array is most likely a UTF-8 encoded String containing a line of text.

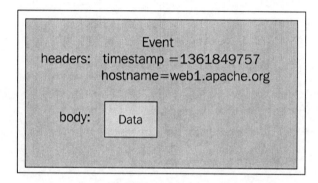

Flume may add additional headers automatically (for example, when a source adds the hostname where the data is sourced or creating an event's timestamp), but the body is mostly untouched unless you edit it en-route using interceptors.

Interceptors, channel selectors, and sink processors

An **interceptor** is a point in your data flow where you can inspect and alter Flume **events**. You can chain zero or more interceptors after a **source** creates an **event** or before a **sink** sends the **event** wherever it is destined. If you are familiar with the AOP Spring Framework, it is similar to a `MethodInterceptor`. In Java Servlets it is similar to a `ServletFilter`. Here's an example of what using four chained interceptors on a source might look like:

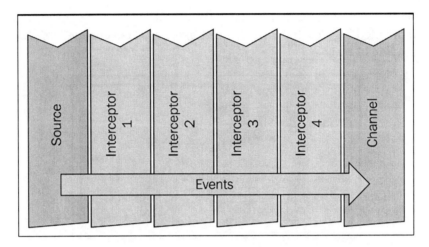

Channel selectors are responsible for how data moves from a source to one or more channels. Flume comes packaged with two channel selectors, which cover most use cases you might have, although you can write your own if needed. A replicating channel selector (the default) simply puts a copy of the event into each channel assuming you have configured more than one. In contrast, a multiplexing channel selector can write to different channels depending on certain header information. Combined with Interceptor logic, this duo forms the foundation for routing input to different channels.

Finally, a sink processor is the mechanism by which you can create failover paths for your sinks or load balance events across multiple sinks from a channel.

Tiered data collection (multiple flows and/or agents)

You can chain your Flume agents depending on your particular use case. For example, you may want to insert an agent in a tiered fashion to limit the number of clients trying to connect directly to your Hadoop cluster. More likely your source machines don't have sufficient disk space to deal with a prolonged outage or maintenance window, so you create a tier with lots of disk space between your sources and your Hadoop cluster.

In the following diagram you can see there are two places data is created (on the left) and two final destinations for the data (the **HDFS** and **ElasticSearch** cloud bubbles on the right). To make things more interesting, let's say one of the machines generates two kinds of data (let's call them square and triangle data). You can see in the lower-left agent we use a multiplexing channel selector to split the two kinds of data into different channels. The rectangle channel is then routed to the agent in the upper-right corner (along with the data coming from the upper-left agent). The combined volume of events is written together in HDFS in datacenter 1. Meanwhile the triangle data is sent to the agent that writes to ElasticSearch in datacenter 2. Keep in mind that the data transformations can occur after any source or before any sink. How all of these components can be used to build complicated data workflows will become clear as the book proceeds.

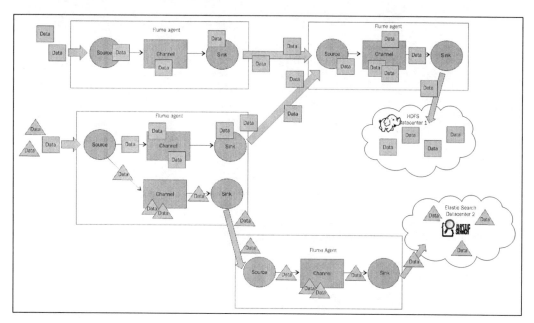

Summary

In this chapter we discussed the problem that Flume is attempting to solve; getting data into your Hadoop cluster for data processing in an easily configured and reliable way. We also discussed the Flume agent and its logical components including: events, sources, channel selectors, channels, sink processors, and sinks.

The next chapter will cover these in more detail, specifically the most commonly used implementations of each. Like all good open source projects, almost all of these components are extensible if the bundled ones don't do what you need them to do.

2
Flume Quick Start

As we covered some basics in the previous chapter, this chapter will help you get started with Flume. So, let us start with the first step, downloading and configuring Flume.

Downloading Flume

Let's download Flume from `http://flume.apache.org/`. Look for the download link in the side navigation. You'll see two compressed tar archives, available along with checksum and gpg signature files used to verify the archives. Instructions for verifying the download are on the website so I won't cover them here. Checking the checksum file contents against the actual checksum verifies that the download was not corrupted. Checking the signature file validates that all the files you are downloading (including the checksum and signature) came from Apache and not someplace nefarious. Do you really need to verify your downloads? In general it is a good idea and it is recommended by Apache that you do so. If you choose not to, I won't tell.

The binary distribution archive has `bin` in the name and the source archive is marked with `src`. The source archive contains just the Flume source code. The binary distribution is much larger because it contains not just the Flume source and the compiled Flume components (JARs, javadocs, and so on), but all the dependent Java libraries as well. The binary package contains the same Maven POM file as the source archive so you can always recompile the code even if you start with the binary distribution.

Go ahead and download (and verify) the binary distribution to save us some time in getting started.

Flume in Hadoop distributions

Flume is available with some Hadoop distributions. The distributions supposedly provide bundles of Hadoop's core components and satellite projects (such as Flume) in a way that things such as version compatibility and additional bug fixes have been taken into account. These distributions aren't better or worse, just different.

There are benefits to using a distribution. Someone else has already done the work of pulling together all the version compatible components. Today this is less of an issue since the Apache Bigtop project started (`http://bigtop.apache.org/`). Nevertheless, having prebuilt standard OS packages such as RPMs and DEBs eases installation as well as providing startup/shutdown scripts. Each distribution has different levels of free to paid options including paid professional services if you really get into a situation you just can't handle.

There are downsides, of course. The version of Flume bundled in a distribution will often lag quite a bit behind the Apache releases. If there is a new or bleeding-edge feature you are interested in using, you'll either be waiting for your distribution's provider to backport it for you or you'll be stuck patching it yourself. Furthermore, while the distribution providers do a fair amount of testing, like any general purpose platform, you will most likely encounter something that their testing didn't cover. In this case you are still on the hook to come up with a workaround or to dive into the code, fix it, and hopefully submit that patch back to the open source community (where at some future point it'll make it into an update of your distribution or the next version).

So things move slower in a Hadoop distribution world. You may see that as good or bad. Usually large companies don't like the instability of bleeding-edge technology or making changes often, as change can be the most common cause of unplanned outages. You'd be hard pressed to find such a company using the bleeding-edge Linux kernel rather than something like **Red Hat Enterprise Linux** (**RHEL**), CentOS, Ubuntu LTS, or any of the other distributions that aim for is stability and compatibility. If you are a startup building the next Internet fad, you might need that bleeding-edge feature to get a leg up on the established competition.

If you are considering a distribution, do the research and see what you are getting (or not getting) with each. Remember each of these offerings is hoping that you'll eventually want and/or need their Enterprise offering, which usually doesn't come cheap. Do your homework.

> Here's a short and non-definitive list of some of the more established players for more information:
> - Cloudera: `http://cloudera.com/`
> - Hortonworks: `http://hortonworks.com/`
> - MapR: `http://mapr.com/`

Flume configuration file overview

Now that we've downloaded Flume, let's spend some time going over how to configure an agent.

A Flume agent's default configuration provider uses a simple Java property file of key/value pairs that you pass as an argument to the agent upon startup. Since you can configure more than one agent in a single file, you will need to additionally pass an agent identifier (called a name) so it knows which configurations to use. In my examples where I'm only specifying one agent I'm going to use the name `agent`.

Each agent is configured starting with three parameters:

```
agent.sources=<list of sources>
agent.channels=<list of channels>
agent.sinks=<list of sinks>
```

Each source, channel, and sink also has a unique name within the context of that agent. For example, if I'm going to transport my Apache access logs, I might define a channel named `access`. The configurations for this channel would all start with the prefix `agent.channels.access`. Each configuration item has a type property that tells Flume what kind of source, channel, or sink it is. In this case, we are going to use an in-memory channel whose type is `memory`. The complete configuration for the channel named `access` in the agent named `agent` would be as follows:

```
agent.channels.access.type=memory
```

Any arguments to a source, channel, or sink are added as additional properties using the same prefix. The memory channel has a capacity parameter to indicate the maximum number of Flume events it can hold. Let's say we didn't want to use the default value of 100; our configuration would now look as follows:

```
agent.channels.access.type=memory
agent.channels.access.capacity=200
```

Finally, we need to add the access channel name to the agent.channels property so the agent knows to load it:

```
agent.channels=access
```

Let's look at a complete example using the canonical "Hello World" example.

Starting up with "Hello World"

No technical book would be complete without a "Hello World" example. Here is the configuration file we'll be using:

```
agent.sources=s1
agent.channels=c1
agent.sinks=k1
agent.sources.s1.type=netcat
agent.sources.s1.channels=c1
agent.sources.s1.bind=0.0.0.0
agent.sources.s1.port=12345
agent.channels.c1.type=memory
agent.sinks.k1.type=logger
agent.sinks.k1.channel=c1
```

Here I've defined one agent (called agent) that has a source named s1, a channel named c1, and a sink named k1.

The s1 source's type is netcat, which simply opens a socket listening for events (one line of text per event). It requires two parameters, a bind IP and a port number. In this example we are using 0.0.0.0 for a bind address (the Java convention to specify listen on any address) and port 12345. The source configuration also has a parameter called channels (plural) that is the name of the channel/channels the source will append events to, in this case c1. It is plural, because you can configure a source to write to more than one channel; we just aren't doing that in this simple example.

The channel named c1 is a memory channel with default configuration.

The sink named `k1` is of type `logger`. This is a sink that is mostly used for debugging and testing. It will log all events at INFO level using log4j, which it receives from the configured channel, in this case `c1`. Here the channel keyword is singular because a sink can only be fed data from one channel.

Using this configuration, let's run the agent and connect to it using the Linux netcat utility to send an event.

First, explode the `tar` archive of the binary distribution we downloaded earlier:

```
$ tar -zxf apache-flume-1.3.1.tar.gz
$ cd apache-flume-1.3.1
```

Next, let's briefly look at the `help` command. Run the `flume-ng` command with the `help` command:

```
$ ./bin/flume-ng help
Usage: ./bin/flume-ng<command> [options]...


commands:
  help                    display this help text
agent                   run a Flume agent
avro-client             run an avro Flume client
version                 show Flume version info


global options:
--conf,-c <conf>        use configs in <conf> directory
  --classpath,-C <cp>   append to the classpath
--dryrun,-d             do not actually start Flume, just print the command
-Dproperty=value        sets a JDK system property value


agent options:
--conf-file,-f <file> specify a config file (required)
--name,-n <name>        the name of this agent (required)
--help,-h               display help text
```

```
avro-client options:
--dirname<dir>        directory to stream to avro source
--host,-H <host>      hostname to which events will be sent (required)
--port,-p <port>      port of the avro source (required)
--filename,-F <file>  text file to stream to avro source [default: std
input]
--headerFile,-R <file>headerFile containing headers as key/value pairs on
each
```

```
new line
  --help,-h               display help text
```

 Note that if the <conf> directory is specified, then it is always included first in the classpath.

As you can see, there are two ways you can invoke the command (other than the trivial `help` and `version` commands). We will be using the `agent` command. The use of `avro-client` will be covered later.

The `agent` command has two required parameters, a configuration file to use and the agent name (in case your configuration contains multiple agents). Let's take our sample configuration and open an editor (`vi` in my case, but use whatever you like):

```
$ vi conf/hw.conf
```

Next, place the contents of the `vi` configuration into the editor, save, and exit back to the shell.

Now you can start the agent:

```
$ ./bin/flume-ng agent -n agent -c conf -f conf/hw.conf
-Dflume.root.logger=INFO,console
```

The `-Dflume.root.logger` property overrides the root logger in `conf/log4j.properties` to use the `console` appender. If we didn't override the root logger, everything would still work, but the output would be going to a file `log/flume.log` instead. Of course, you can also just edit the `conf/log4j.properties` file and change the `flume.root.logger` property (or anything else you like).

You might ask why you need to specify the -c parameter since the -f parameter contains the complete relative path to the configuration. The reason for this is the log4j configuration file would be included on the classpath. If you left the -c parameter off that command you'd see the following error:

```
log4j:WARN No appenders could be found for logger
  (org.apache.flume.lifecycle.LifecycleSupervisor).
  log4j:WARN Please initialize the log4j system properly.
  log4j:WARN See
  http://logging.apache.org/log4j/1.2/faq.html#noconfig for more
  info.
```

But you didn't do that so you should see the following key log lines:

```
2013-03-03 12:26:47,437 (main) [INFO -
  org.apache.flume.node.FlumeNode.start(FlumeNode.java:54)] Flume
  node starting - agent
```

This line tells you that your agent is starting with the name agent. Usually you'd only look for this line to be sure you started the right configuration when you have multiples defined in your configuration file:

```
2013-03-03 12:26:47,448 (conf-file-poller-0) [INFO -
  org.apache.flume.conf.file.
  AbstractFileConfigurationProvider$FileWatcherRunnable.run
  (AbstractFileConfigurationProvider.java:195)] Reloading
  configuration file:conf/hw.conf
```

This is another sanity check to make sure you are loading the correct file, in this case the hw.conf file:

```
2013-03-03 12:26:47,516 (conf-file-poller-0) [INFO -
  org.apache.flume.node.nodemanager.DefaultLogicalNodeManager.
  startAllComponents(DefaultLogicalNodeManager.java:106)] Starting
  new configuration:{ sourceRunners:{s1=EventDrivenSourceRunner: {
  source:org.apache.flume.source.NetcatSource{name:s1,state:IDLE}
  }} sinkRunners:{k1=SinkRunner: {
  policy:org.apache.flume.sink
  .DefaultSinkProcessor@42552ccounterGroup:{ name:null counters:{}
  } }} channels:{c1=org.apache.flume.channel.MemoryChannel{name:
  c1}} }
```

Once all the configurations have been parsed you see this message, which shows everything that was configured. You can see s1, c1, and k1 and which Java classes are actually doing the work. As you probably guessed, netcat is a convenience for org.apache.flume.source.NetcatSource. We could have used the classname if we wanted. In fact, if I had my own custom source written, I would use its classname for the source's type parameter. You cannot define your own short names without patching the Flume distribution:

```
2013-03-03 12:26:48,045 (lifecycleSupervisor-1-1) [INFO -
   org.apache.flume.source.NetcatSource.start
   (NetcatSource.java:164)] Created
   serverSocket:sun.nio.ch.ServerSocketChannelImpl[/0.0.0.0:12345]
```

Here we see that our source is now listening on port 12345 for input. So let's send it some data.

Finally, open a second terminal. We'll use the nc command (you can use telnet or something similar) to send the String "Hello World" and click on <RETURN> to mark the end of the event:

```
% nclocalhost 12345
   Hello World<RETURN>
   OK
```

"OK" came from the agent after pressing return signifying it accepted the line of text as a single Flume event. If you look at the agent log you see the following:

```
2013-03-03 12:39:58,582 (SinkRunner-PollingRunner-
   DefaultSinkProcessor) [INFO -
   org.apache.flume.sink.LoggerSink.process(LoggerSink.java:70)]
   Event: { headers:{} body: 48 65 6C6C6F 20 57 6F 72 6C 64
   Hello World }
```

This log message shows that the Flume event contains no headers (netcat source doesn't add any itself). The body is shown in hexadecimal along with a String representation (for us humans to read, in this case the Hello World message).

If I send another line as follows:

```
The quick brown fox jumped over the lazy dog.<RETURN>
   OK
```

You'll see the following in the agent's log:

```
2013-03-03 12:45:08,466 (SinkRunner-PollingRunner-
   DefaultSinkProcessor) [INFO -
   org.apache.flume.sink.LoggerSink.process(LoggerSink.java:70)]
   Event: { headers:{} body: 54 68 65 20 71 75 69 63 6B 20 62 72 6F
   77 6E 20 The quick brown  }
```

The event appears to have been truncated. The logger sink, by design, limits the body content to 16 bytes to avoid your screen from being filled with more than what you'd need in a debugging context. If you need to see the full contents for debugging, you should use a different sink, perhaps the `file_roll` sink, which will write to the local filesystem.

Summary

In this chapter we covered downloading the Flume binary distribution. We created a simple configuration file that included one source writing to one channel feeding one sink. The source listened on a socket for network clients to connect and send it event data. Those events were written to an in-memory channel and then fed to a log4j sink to become output. We then connected to our listening agent using the Linux netcat utility and sent some String events into our Flume agent's source. Finally, we verified that our log4j based sink wrote the events out.

In the next chapter we'll take a detailed look at the two major channel types you'll likely use in your data processing workflows:

- Memory channel
- File channel

For each type we'll discuss all the configuration knobs available to you, when and why you might want to deviate from the defaults, and, most importantly, why to use one over the other.

3
Channels

In Flume, a channel is the construct used between sources and sinks. It provides a holding area for your in-flight events after they are read from sources until they can be written to sinks in your data processing pipelines.

The two types we'll cover here are a memory-backed/non-durable channel and a local filesystem backed/durable channel. The durable file channel flushes all changes to disk before acknowledging receipt of the event to the sender. This is considerably slower than using the non-durable memory channel, but provides recoverability in the event of system or Flume agent restarts. Conversely, the memory channel is much faster, but failure results in data loss and has much lower storage capacity when compared with the multi-terabyte disks backing the file channel. Which channel you choose depends on your specific use cases, failure scenarios, and risk tolerance.

That said, regardless of what channel you choose, if your rate of ingest from the sources into the channel is greater than the rate the sink can write data, you will exceed the capacity of the channel and you will throw a ChannelException. What your source does or doesn't do with that ChannelException is source specific, but in some cases data loss is possible so you'll want to avoid filling channels by sizing things properly. In fact, you always want your sink to be able to write faster than your source input. Otherwise, you may get into a situation where once your sink falls behind you can never catch up. If your data volume tracks with site usage, you may have higher volumes during the day and lower volumes at night, giving your channels time to drain. In practice, you'll want to try and keep the channel depth (the number of events currently in the channel) as low as possible because time spent in the channel translates to a time delay before reaching the final destination.

Memory channel

A memory channel, as expected, is a channel where in-flight events are stored in memory. Since memory is (usually) orders of magnitude faster than disk, events can be ingested much more quickly resulting in reduced hardware needs. The downside of using this channel is that an agent failure (hardware problem, power outage, JVM crash, Flume restart, and so on) results in loss of data. Depending on your use case, this may be perfectly fine. System metrics usually fall into this category as a few lost data points isn't the end of the world. However, if your events represent purchases on your website, then a memory channel would be a poor choice.

To use the memory channel, set the `type` parameter on your named channel to `memory`.

```
agent.channels.c1.type=memory
```

This defines a memory channel named `c1` for the agent named `agent`.

Here is a table of configuration parameters you can adjust from the default values:

Key	Required	Type	Default
type	Yes	String	memory
capacity	No	int	100
transactionCapacity	No	int	100
byteCapacityBufferPercentage	No	int (percent)	20%
byteCapacity	No	long (bytes)	80% of JVM Heap
keep-alive	No	int	3 (seconds)

The default capacity of this channel is 100 Events. This can be adjusted by setting the `capacity` property as follows:

```
agent.channels.c1.capacity=200
```

Remember if you increase this value you may also have to increase your Java heap space using the `-Xmx` and optionally the `-Xms` parameters.

Another capacity related setting you can set is `transactionCapacity`. This is the maximum number of events that can be written, also called a put, by a source's `ChannelProcessor`, the component responsible for moving data from the source to the channel in a single transaction. This is also the number of events that can be read, also called a take, in a single transaction by `SinkProcessor`, the component responsible for moving data from the channel to the sink. You may want to set this higher to decrease the overhead of the transaction wrapper, which may speed things up. The downside to increasing this, in the event of a failure, is that a source would have to roll back more data.

Flume only provides transactional guarantees for each channel in each individual agent. In a multiagent, multi-channel configuration duplicates and out of order delivery are likely but should not be considered the norm. If you are getting duplicates in non-failure conditions, it means you need to continue tuning your Flume configurations.

If you are using a sink that writes someplace that benefits from larger batches of work (such as HDFS), you might want to set this higher. Like many things, the only way to be sure is to run performance tests with different values. The blog post `http://bit.ly/flumePerfPt1` from Flume committer Mike Percy should give you some good starting points.

The `byteCapacityBufferPercentage` and `byteCapacity` parameters were introduced in `https://issues.apache.org/jira/browse/FLUME-1535` as a means of sizing memory channel capacity using bytes used rather than the number of events, as well as trying to avoid `OutOfMemoryErrors`. If your Events have a large variance in size, you may be tempted to use these settings to adjust capacity, but be warned that calculations are estimated from the event's body only. If you have any headers, which you will, your actual memory usage will be higher than the configured values.

Finally, the `keep-alive` parameter is the time the thread writing data into the channel will wait when the channel is full before giving up. Since data is being drained from the channel at the same time, if space opens up before the timeout expires, the data will be written to the channel rather than throwing an exception back to the source. You may be tempted to set this value very high, but remember that waiting for a write to a channel will block data flowing into your source, which may cause data backing up in an upstream agent. Eventually, this may result in events being dropped. You need to size for periodic spikes in traffic as well as temporary planned (and unplanned) maintenance.

File channel

A file channel is a channel that stores events to the local filesystem of the agent. While slower than the memory channel, it provides a durable storage path that can survive most issues, and should be used in use cases where a gap in your data flow is undesirable.

This durability is provided by a combination of a **Write Ahead Log (WAL)** and one or more file storage directories. The WAL is used to track all input and output from the channel in an atomically safe way. In this way, if the agent is restarted, the WAL can be replayed to make sure all the events that came into the channel (puts) have been written out (takes) before the storage of the data can be purged from the local filesystem.

Additionally, the file channel supports encrypting data written to the filesystem should your data handling policy require that all data on disk (even temporarily) be encrypted. I won't cover this here, but if you need it, there is an example in the Flume User Guide (`http://flume.apache.org/FlumeUserGuide.html`). Keep in mind that using encryption will reduce the throughput of your file channel.

To use the file channel, set the `type` parameter on your named channel to `file`:

```
agent.channels.c1.type=file
```

This defines a file channel named `c1` for the agent named `agent`.

Here is a table of configuration parameters you can adjust from the default values:

Key	Required	Type	Default
type	Yes	String	file
checkpointDir	No	String	~/.flume/file-channel/checkpoint
dataDirs	No	String (comma-separated list)	~/.flume/file-channel/data
capacity	No	int	1000000
keep-alive	No	int	3 (seconds)
transactionCapacity	No	int	1000
checkpointInterval	No	long	300000 (milliseconds - 5 min)
write-timeout	No	int	10 (seconds)
maxFileSize	No	long	2146435071 (bytes)
minimumRequiredSpace	No	long	524288000 (bytes)

To specify the location where the Flume agent should hold data, you set the `checkpointDir` and `dataDirs` properties:

```
agent.channels.c1.checkpointDir=/flume/c1/checkpoint
agent.channels.c1.dataDirs=/flume/c1/data
```

Technically, these properties are not required and have sensible defaults for development. However, if you have more than one file channel configured in your agent, only the first channel will start. For production deployments and development work with multiple file channels, you should use distinct directory paths for each file channel storage area, and consider placing different channels on different disks to avoid IO contention. Additionally, if you are sizing a large machine consider using some form of RAID that contains striping (RAID 10, 50, 60) to achieve higher disk performance rather than buying more expensive 10k or 15k drives or SSDs. If you don't have RAID striping but do have multiple disks, set `dataDirs` to a comma separated list of each storage location. Using multiple disks will spread the disk traffic almost as well as striped RAID, but without the computational overhead associated with RAID 50/60 as well as the 50% space waste associated with RAID 10. You'll want to test your system to see if the RAID overhead is worth the speed difference. Since hard drive failures are a reality, you may prefer certain RAID configurations to single disks in order to isolate yourself from the data loss associated with single drive failures.

NFS storage should be avoided for the same reason. Using the JDBC channel is a bad idea as it would introduce a bottleneck and single point of failure instead of what should be designed as a highly distributed system.

Be sure you set the `HADOOP_PREFIX` and `JAVA_HOME` environment variables when using the file channel. While we seemingly haven't used anything Hadoop specific (such as writing to HDFS), the file channel uses Hadoop `Writeables` as an on-disk serialization format. If Flume can't find the Hadoop libraries you might see this in your startup so check your environment variables:

```
java.lang.NoClassDefFoundError: org/apache/hadoop/
io/Writable
```

The default file channel `capacity` is one million events, regardless of size of the event contents. If the channel capacity is reached, a source will no longer be able to ingest data. This default should be fine for low volume cases. You'll want to size this higher if your ingestion is heavy enough that you can't tolerate normal planned or unplanned outages. For instance, there are many configuration changes you can make in Hadoop that require a cluster restart. If you have Flume writing important data into Hadoop, the file channel should be sized to tolerate the time it takes to restart Hadoop (and maybe add a comfort buffer for the unexpected). If your cluster or other systems are unreliable, you can set this higher to handle even larger amounts of downtime. At some point you'll run into the fact that your disk space is a finite resource, so you will have to pick some upper limit (or buy bigger disks).

The keep-alive parameter is similar to the memory channel's. It is the maximum time the source will wait when trying to write into a full channel before giving up. If space becomes available before the timeout, the write is successful; otherwise a ChannelException is thrown back to the source.

The property transactionCapacity is the maximum number of events allowed in a single transaction. This may become important with certain sources that batch together events and pass them to the channel in a single call. Most likely you won't need to change this from the default. Setting this higher allocates additional resources internally so you shouldn't increase it unless you run into performance issues.

The checkpointInterval property is the number of milliseconds between performing a checkpoint (which also rolls the log files written to logDirs). You cannot set this lower than 1000 milliseconds.

Checkpoint files are also roll based on volume of data written to them using the maxFileSize property. You can lower this value for low traffic channels if you want to try and save some disk space. Let's say your maximum file size is 50,000 bytes but your channel only writes 500 bytes a day, it would take 100 days to fill a single log. Let's say that you were on day #100 and 2000 bytes came in all at once. Some data would be written to the old file and a new file would get started with the overflow. After the roll, Flume tries to remove any log files that aren't needed anymore. Since the full log has unprocessed records, it cannot be removed yet. The next chance to clean up that old log file may not come for another 100 days. It probably doesn't matter if that old 50,000 byte file sticks around longer, but since the default is around 2 GB, you could have twice that (4 GB) disk space used per channel. Depending on how much available disk you have, and the number of channels configured in your agent, this may or may not be a problem. If your machines have plenty of storage space, the default should be fine.

Finally, the minimumRequiredSpace property is the amount of space you do not want to use for writing of logs. The default configuration will throw an exception if you attempt to use the last 500 MB of the disk associated with the dataDir path. This limit applies across all channels, so if you have three file channels configured, the upper limit is still 500 MB, not 1.5 GB. You can set this as value as low as 1 MB, but, generally speaking, bad things tend to happen when you push disk utilization towards 100%.

Summary

In this chapter we covered the two channel types you are most likely to use in your data processing pipelines.

The memory channel offers speed at the cost of data loss in the event of failure.

Alternatively, the file channel provides a more reliable transport, in that it can tolerate agent failures and restarts, at a performance cost.

You will need to decide which channel is appropriate for your use cases. When trying to decide if a memory channel is appropriate, ask yourself what is the monetary cost if you lose some data. Weigh that against the additional costs of more hardware to cover the difference in performance when deciding if you need a durable channel after all. Another consideration is whether or not the data could be resent. Not all data you may ingest into Hadoop will come from streaming application logs. If you receive daily downloads of data, you can get away with using a memory channel because if you encounter a problem, you can always rerun the import.

> Possible (or intentional) duplicate events are a fact of ingesting streaming data. Some people will run periodic MapReduce jobs to clean the data (and removing duplicates while they are at it). Others will just account for duplicates when they run their MapReduce jobs, which saves additional post processing. In practice you will probably do both.

In the next chapter, we'll look at sinks, specifically, the HDFS sink for writing events to HDFS. We will also cover event serializers, which specify how Flume Events are translated into output more suitable for the sink. Finally, we will cover sink processors and how to set up load balancing and failure paths in a tiered configuration for a more robust data transport.

4
Sinks and Sink Processors

By now you should have a pretty good idea where the sink fits into the Flume architecture. In this chapter we will learn about the most used sink with Hadoop, the HDFS sink. The general architecture of Flume supports many other sinks we won't have space to cover all of them in this book. Some come bundled with Flume that can write to HBase, IRC, ElasticSearch, and as we saw in *Chapter 2*, *Flume Quick Start*, a log4j and file sink. Other sinks are available on the Internet that can be used to write data to MongoDB, Cassandra, RabbitMQ, Redis, and just about any other data store you can think of. If you can't find a sink that suits your needs, you could write one easily by extending the `org.apache.flume.sink.Abstractsink` class.

HDFS sink

The job of the HDFS sink is to continuously open a file in HDFS, stream data into it, and at some point close that file and start a new one. As we discussed in *Chapter 1*, *Overview and Architecture*, how long between files rotations must be balanced with how quickly files are closed in HDFS, thus making the data visible for processing. As we've discussed, having lots of tiny files for input will make your MapReduce jobs inefficient.

To use the HDFS sink, set the `type` parameter on your named `sink` to `hdfs`:

```
agent.sinks.k1.type=hdfs
```

This defines a HDFS sink named `k1` for the agent named `agent`. There are some additional required parameters you need to specify, starting with `path` in HDFS where you want to write the data:

```
agent.sinks.k1.hdfs.path=/path/in/hdfs
```

This HDFS path, like most file paths in Hadoop, can be specified in three different ways, namely, absolute, absolute with server name, and relative. These are all equivalent (assuming your Flume Agent is run as the flume user):

Type	Path
absolute	`/Users/flume/mydata`
absolute with server name	`hdfs://namenode/Users/flume/mydata`
relative	`mydata`

I prefer to configure any server I'm installing Flume on with a working `hadoop` command line, by setting the `fs.default.name` property in Hadoop's `core-site.xml` file. I don't keep persistent data in HDFS user directories, but prefer to use absolute paths with some meaningful path name (that is `/logs/apache/access`). The only time I would specify a name node specifically is if the target was a different Hadoop cluster entirely. This allows you to move configurations you've already tested in one environment into another without unintended consequences, such as your production server writing data to your staging Hadoop cluster because somebody forgot to edit the target in the configuration. Externalizing environment specifics is a good best practice to avoid situations like this.

One final required parameter for the HDFS sink, actually any sink, is the channel that it will be doing take operations from. For this, set the `channel` parameter with the channel name to read from:

```
agent.sinks.k1.channel=c1
```

This tells the `k1` sink to read events from the `c1` channel.

The following is an almost complete list of configuration parameters you can adjust from the default values:

Key	Required	Type	Default
`type`	Yes	`String`	hdfs
`channel`	Yes	`String`	
`hdfs.path`	Yes	`String`	
`hdfs.filePrefix`	No	`String`	FlumeData
`hdfs.fileSuffix`	No	`String`	
`hdfs.maxOpenFiles`	No	`long`	5000
`hdfs.round`	No	`Boolean`	false
`hdfs.roundValue`	No	`int`	1

Key	Required	Type	Default
hdfs.roundUnit	No	String (second, minute, or hour)	second
hdfs.timeZone	No	String	Local Time
hdfs.inUsePrefix	No	String	(CDH4.2.0 or Flume 1.4 only)
hdfs.inUseSuffix	No	String	.tmp (CDH4.2.0 or Flume 1.4 only)
hdfs.rollInterval	No	long (seconds)	30 Seconds (0=disable)
hdfs.rollSize	No	long (bytes)	1024 bytes (0=disable)
hdfs.rollCount	No	long	10 (0=disable)
hdfs.batchSize	No	long	100
hdfs.codeC	No	String	

Remember to always check the Flume User Guide for the version you are using at `http://flume.apache.org/`, as things may change between the release of this book and the version you are actually using.

Path and filename

Each time Flume starts a new file at `hdfs.path` in HDFS to write data into, the filename is composed of `hdfs.filePrefix`, a period character, the epoch timestamp the file was started, and optionally, a file suffix specified by the `hdfs.fileSuffix` property (if set). For example, see the following line of code:

```
agent.sinks.k1.hdfs.path=/logs/apache/access
```

This line would result in a file such as `/logs/apache/access/FlumeData.1362945258`.

However, have a look at the following configuration:

```
agent.sinks.k1.hdfs.path=/logs/apache/access
agent.sinks.k1.hdfs.filePrefix=access
agent.sinks.k1.hdfs.fileSuffix=.log
```

In this configuration, your filenames would be more like `/logs/apache/access/access.1362945258.log`.

Over time, the `hdfs.path` directory will get very full so you will want to add some kind of time element into the path to partition the files into subdirectories. Flume supports various time-based escape sequences, such as `%Y` to specify a four digit year. I like using sequences in the form year/month/day/hour (so they sort oldest to newest) so I often use this for a path:

```
agent.sinks.k1.hdfs.path=/logs/apache/access/%Y/%m/%D/%H
```

This says I want a path like `/logs/apache/access/2013/03/10/18/`.

For a complete list of time-based escape sequences, see the Flume User Guide.

Another handy escape sequence mechanism is the ability to use Flume header values in your path. For instance, if there was a header with a key of `logType`, I could split Apache access and error logs into different directories while using the same channel by escaping the header's key as follows:

```
agent.sinks.k1.hdfs.path=/logs/apache/%{logType}/%Y/%m/%D/%H
```

This would result in access logs going to `/logs/apache/access/2013/03/10/18/` and error logs going to `/logs/apache/error/2013/03/10/18/`. However, if I preferred both log types in the same directory path, I could have instead used `logType` in my `hdfs.filePrefix` as follows:

```
agent.sinks.k1.hdfs.path=/logs/apache/%Y/%m/%D/%H
agent.sinks.k1.hdfs.filePrefix=%{logType}
```

Obviously, it is possible for Flume to write to multiple files at once. The property `hdfs.maxOpenFiles` sets the upper limit on how many can be open at once, with a default of 5000. If you exceed this limit, the oldest file still open is closed. Remember that every open file incurs overhead both at the OS level and in the HDFS (NameNode and DataNode connections).

Another set of properties you may find useful allow for rounding down event times at a hour, minute, or second granularity while still maintaining those elements in file paths. Let's say you had a path specification as follows:

```
agent.sinks.k1.hdfs.path=/logs/apache/%Y/%m/%D/%H%M
```

But in this you wanted only four subdirectories per day (at 00, 15, 30, and 45 past the hour, each containing 15 minutes of data). You could accomplish this by setting the following values:

```
agent.sinks.k1.hdfs.round=true
agent.sinks.k1.hdfs.roundValue=15
agent.sinks.k1.hdfs.roundUnit=minute
```

This would result in logs between 01:15:00 and 01:29:59 on 2013-03-10 to be written to files contained in `/logs/apache/2013/03/10/0115/`. Logs from 01:30:00 to 01:44:59 would be written in files contained in `/logs/apache/2013/03/10/0130/`.

The `hdfs.timeZone` property is used to specify the time zone that you want time interpreted for your escape sequences. The default is your computer's local time. If your local time is affected by daylight savings time adjustments, you will have twice as much data when `%H == 02` (in the fall) and no data when `%H == 02` (in the spring). I think it is a bad idea to introduce time zones into things that are meant for computers to read. I believe time zones are a concern for humans alone and computers should only converse in universal time. For this reason I set this property on my Flume agents to make the time zone issue just go away:

```
-Duser.timezone=UTC
```

If you don't agree you are free to use the default (local time), or set `hdfs.timeZone` to whatever you like. The value you passed is used in a call to `java.util.Timezone.getTimeZone(...)` so check the Javadocs for acceptable values to use here.

Finally, while files are being written to the HDFS, a `.tmp` extension is added. When the file is closed, the extension is removed. This allows you to easily exclude these files as input when running a MapReduce job on a directory actively being written to by Flume. It also allows you to see which files are being written to by looking at a directory listing in HDFS. Since you typically specify a directory for input in your MapReduce job (or because you are using Hive), the temporary files will often be picked up by mistake as empty or garbled input. FLUME-1702 was created to address this and will be released in Flume 1.4, but if you happen to be using Cloudera's CDH4.2.0 release, the change was backported into Flume 1.3. This introduces two new properties to change the "in use" prefix and suffix. To avoid having your temporary files picked up before being closed, set the suffix to blank (rather than the default of `.tmp`) and the prefix to either a dot or an underscore character as follows:

```
agent.sinks.k1.hdfs.inUsePrefix=_
agent.sinks.k1.hdfs.inUseSuffix=
```

File rotation

By default, Flume will rotate actively written to files every 30 seconds, 10 events, or 1024 bytes. This is done by setting the `hdfs.rollInterval`, `hdfs.rollCount`, and `hdfs.rollSize` properties respectively. One or more of these can be set to zero to disable that particular rolling mechanism. For instance, if you only wanted a time based roll of 1 minute, you would set these parameters as follows:

```
agent.sinks.k1.hdfs.rollInterval=60
agent.sinks.k1.hdfs.rollCount=0
agent.sinks.k1.hdfs.rollSize=0
```

If your output contains any amount of header information, the HDFS size per file may be larger than what you expect because the hdfs.rollSize rotation scheme only counts the event body length. Clearly you may not want to disable all three mechanisms for rotation at the same time or you will have one directory in the HDFS overflowing with files.

Finally, a related parameter is hdfs.batchSize. This is the number of events that the sink will read per transaction from the channel. If you have a large volume of data in your channel, you may see a performance increase by setting this higher than the default of 100, which decreases the transaction overhead per event.

Now that we've discussed the way files are managed and rolled in HDFS, let's look into how the event content gets written.

Compression codecs

Codecs (coder/decoders) are used to compress and decompress data using various compression algorithms. gzip, bzip2, lzo, and snappy are supported by Flume, although you may have to install lzo yourself, especially if you are using a distribution such as CDH due to licensing issues.

If you want to specify compression for your data, you set the hdfs.codeC property if you want the HDFS sink to write compressed files. The property is also used as the file suffix for the files written to HDFS. For example, if you specify the codec as follows all files written will have a .gzip extension, so you don't need to specify a hdfs.fileSuffix property in this case:

```
agent.sinks.k1.hdfs.codeC=gzip
```

Which codec you choose to use will require some research on your part. There are arguments for using gzip or bzip2 for their higher compression ratios at the cost of longer compression times, especially if your data is written once but will be read hundreds or thousands of times. On the other hand, using snappy or lzo results in faster compression performance, but results in a lower compression ratio. Keep in mind that splittability of the file, especially if you are using plain text files, will greatly affect the performance of your MapReduce jobs. Go pick up a copy of *Hadoop Beginner's Guide* (http://amzn.to/14Dh6TA) or *Hadoop: The Definitive Guide* (http://amzn.to/16OsfIf) if you aren't sure what I'm talking about.

Event serializers

An event serializer is the mechanism by which a Flume event is converted into another format for output. It is similar in function to the `Layout` class in log4j. By default, the `text` serializer, which outputs just the Flume event body. There is another, `header_and_text`, which outputs both the headers and the body. Finally, there is an `avro_event` serializer that can be used to create an Avro representation of the event. If you write your own, you'd use the implementation's fully qualified class name as the `serializer` property value.

Text output

As mentioned previously, the default serializer is the `text` serializer. This will output only the Flume event body, with the headers discarded. Each event has a new line character appender unless you override this default behavior by setting the `serializer.appendNewLine` property to `false`.

Key	Required	Type	Default
serializer	No	String	text
serializer.appendNewLine	No	boolean	true

Text with headers

The `text_with_headers` serializer allows you to save the Flume event headers rather than discarding them. The output format consists of the headers, followed by a space, then the body payload, and finally terminated by an optionally disabled new line character. Here is some example output produced by this serializer:

```
{key1=value1, key2=value2} body text here
```

Key	Required	Type	Default
serializer	No	String	text_with_headers
serializer.appendNewLine	No	boolean	true

Apache Avro

The Apache Avro project (http://avro.apache.org/) provides a serialization format similar in functionality to Google protocol buffers, but is more Hadoop friendly as the container is based on HadoopSequenceFiles and has some MapReduce integration. The format is also self-describing using JSON, making for a good long-term data storage format, as your data format may evolve over time. If your data has a lot of structure that you want to avoid turning into Strings, only to then parse those Strings in your MapReduce job, you should go read more about Avro to see if you want to use it as a storage format in HDFS.

The avro_event serializer creates Avro data based on the Flume event schema. It has no formatting parameters, since Avro dictates the format of the data and the structure of the Flume event dictates the schema used:

Key	Required	Type	Default
serializer	No	String	avro_event
serializer.compressionCodec	No	String (gzip, bzip2, lzo, or snappy)	
serializer.syncIntervalBytes	No	int (bytes)	2048000 (bytes)

If you want to use Avro, but want to use a different schema from the Flume event schema, you will have to write your own event serializer.

If you want your data compressed before being written to the Avro container, you should set the serializer.compressionCodec property to the file extension of an installed codec. The serializer.syncIntervalBytes property determines the size of the data buffer used before flushing the data to HDFS, and therefore, this setting can affect your compression ratio when using a codec. Here is an example using snappy compression on Avro data using a 4 MB buffer:

```
agent.sinks.k1.serializer=avro_event
agent.sinks.k1.serializer.compressionCodec=snappy
agent.sinks.k1.serializer.syncIntervalBytes=4194304
agent.sinks.k1.hdfs.fileSuffix=.avro
```

For Avro files to work in an Avro MapReduce job, they must end in .avro or they will be ignored as input. For this reason, you need to explicitly set the hdfs.fileSuffix property. Furthermore, you would not set the hdfs.codeC property on an Avro file.

File type

By default the HDFS sink writes data to HDFS as Hadoop SequenceFiles. This is a common Hadoop wrapper that consists of a key and value field separated by binary field and record delimiters. Usually, text files on a computer make assumptions like a newline character terminates each record. So what do you do if your data contains a newline character, like some XML? Using a sequence file can solve this problem because it uses non-printable characters for delimiters. SequenceFiles are also splittable which makes for better locality and parallelism when running MapReduce jobs on your data, especially on large files.

Sequence file

When using a SequenceFile file type, you need to specify how you want the key and value to be written on the record in the SequenceFile. The key on each record will always be a `LongWritable` containing the current timestamp or if the timestamp event header is set, will be used instead. By default, the format of the value is a `org.apache.hadoop.io.BytesWritable` that corresponds with the `byte[]` Flume body:

Key	Required	Type	Default
hdfs.fileType	No	String	SequenceFile
hdfs.writeType	No	String	writable

However, if you want the payload interpreted as a `String`, you can override the `hdfs.writeType` property so a `org.apache.hadoop.io.Text` will be used as the value field:

Key	Required	Type	Default
hdfs.fileType	No	String	SequenceFile
hdfs.writeType	No	String	text

Data stream

If you do not want to output a SequenceFile because your data doesn't have a natural key, you can use a DataStream to output only the value, uncompressed. Simply override the `hdfs.fileType` property:

```
agent.sinks.k1.hdfs.fileType=DataStream
```

This is the file type you would use with Avro serialization since any compression should have been done in the event serializer. To serialize `gzip` compressed Avro files you would set the following properties:

```
agent.sinks.k1.serializer=avro_event
agent.sinks.k1.serializer.compressionCodec=gzip
agent.sinks.k1.hdfs.fileType=DataStream
agent.sinks.k1.hdfs.fileSuffix=.avro
```

Compressed stream

The `CompressedStream` is similar to a `DataStream` except that the data is compressed when written. You can think of this as running the `gzip` utility on an uncompressed file, but all in one step. This differs from a compressed Avro file whose contents are compressed and then written into an uncompressed Avro wrapper.

```
agent.sinks.k1.hdfs.fileType=CompressedStream
```

Remember that only certain compressed formats are splittable in MapReduce, should you decide to use a `CompressedStream`. The compression algorithm selection doesn't have a Flume configuration but is instead dictated by the `zlib.compress.strategy` and `zlib.compress.level` properties in core Hadoop.

Timeouts and workers

Finally, there are two miscellaneous properties related to timeouts and two for worker pools that you can change:

Key	Required	Type	Default
hdfs.callTimeout	No	long (milliseconds)	10000
hdfs.idleTimeout	No	int (seconds)	0 (0 = disable)
hdfs.threadsPoolSize	No	int	10
hdfs.rollTimerPoolSize	No	int	1

The `hdfs.callTimeout` is the amount of time the HDFS sink will wait for HDFS operations to return a success (or failure) before giving up. If your Hadoop cluster is particularly slow (for instance a development or virtual cluster) you may need to set this value higher to avoid errors. Keep in mind that your channel will overflow if you cannot sustain higher write throughput than input rate to your channel.

The `hdfs.idleTimeout` property if set to a non-zero value, is the time Flume will wait to automatically close an idle file. I have never used this since `hdfs.fileRollInterval` handles closing of files each roll period and if the channel is idle it will not open a new file. This setting seems to have been created as an alternative roll mechanism to the size, time, and event count mechanisms already discussed. You may want as much data written to a file as possible and only close it when there is really no more data. In this case you can use `hdfs.idleTimeout` to accomplish this rotation scheme if you also set `hdfs.rollInterval`, `hdfs.rollSize`, and `hdfs.rollCount` all to zero.

The first property you can set to adjust the number of workers is `hdfs.threadsPoolSize`, which defaults to 10. This is the maximum number of files that can be written to at the same time. If you are using event headers in determining file paths and names, you may have more than 10 files open at once, but be careful when increasing this value too much so as to not overwhelm the HDFS.

The last property related to worker pools is `hdfs.rollTimerPoolSize`. This is the number of workers processing timeouts set by the `hdfs.idleTimeout` property. The amount of work to close the files is pretty small so increasing this value from the default of one worker is unlikely. If you do not use `hdfs.idleTimeout` based rotation, you can ignore the `hdfs.rollTimerPoolSize` property as it is not used.

Sink groups

In order to remove single points of failure in your data processing pipeline, Flume has the ability to send events to different sinks using either load balancing or failover. In order to do this we need to introduce a new concept called a sink group. A sink group is used to create a logical grouping of sinks. The behavior of this grouping is dictated by something called the sink processor, which determines how events are routed.

There is a default sink processor that contains a single sink that is used whenever you have a sink that isn't part of any sink group. Our Hello World example in *Chapter 2, Flume Quick Start*, used the default sink processor. No special configuration is necessary for single sinks.

In order for Flume to know about the sink groups, there is a new top-level agent property called `sinkgroups`. Similar to Sources, channels, and sinks, you prefix the property with the agent name as follows:

```
agent.sinkgroups=sg1
```

Here we have defined that there is a sink group called `sg1` for the agent named `agent`.

For each named sink group, you need to specify the sinks it contains using the `sinks` property consisting of a space-delimited list of sink names:

```
agent.sinkgroups.sg1.sinks=k1,k2
```

This defines that sinks `k1` and `k2` are part of sink group `sg1` for the agent named `agent`.

Often sink groups are used in conjunction with tiered movement of data to route around failures. However, they can also be used to write to different Hadoop clusters, since even a well maintained cluster has periodic maintenance.

Load balancing

Continuing the previous example, let's say you want to load balance traffic to `k1` and `k2` evenly. There are some additional properties you need to specify as listed in the following table:

Key	Type	Default
processor.type	String	load_balance
processor.selector	String (round_robin, random)	round_robin
processor.backoff	boolean	false

When you set the `processor.type` to `load_balance`, round robin selection will be used unless otherwise specified by the `processor.selector` property. This can be set to either `round_robin` or `random`. You can also specify your own load balancing selector mechanism, which we won't cover here. Consult the Flume documentation if you need this custom control.

The `processor.backoff` property specifies if an exponential backup should be used when retrying a sink that threw an Exception. The default is `false` which means after a thrown Exception, the sink will be tried again next time its turn is up based on round robin or random selection. If set to `true`, then for each failure the wait time is doubled starting at one second up to a limit of around 18 hours (2^16 seconds).

> At the time of writing, the default for `processor.backoff` in the code is false, but the Flume documentation says true. Save yourself a headache and specify what you want rather than relying on the defaults.

Failover

If you would rather try one sink and if that one fails then try another, then you want to set the `processor.type` to `failover`. Next you'll need to set additional properties to specify the order, by setting the `processor.priority` property followed by the sink name:

Key	Type	Default
processor.type	String	failover
processor.priority.NAME	int	
processor.maxpenality	int (milliseconds)	30000

Let's look at this example:

```
agent.sinkgroups.sg1.sinks=k1,k2,k3
agent.sinkgroups.sg1.processor.type=failover
agent.sinkgroups.sg1.processor.priority.k1=10
agent.sinkgroups.sg1.processor.priority.k2=20
agent.sinkgroups.sg1.processor.priority.k3=20
```

Lower priority numbers come first and in the case of a tie, order is arbitrary. You can use any numbering system that makes sense to you (by ones, fives, tens, whatever). In this example, sink k1 will be tried first and if an Exception is thrown either k2 or k3 will be tried next. If k3 was selected first to try and it failed, k2 will still try. If all sinks in the sink group fail, the transaction with the channel is rolled back.

Finally, `processor.maxPenality` sets an upper limit to an exponential backoff for failed sinks in the group. After the first failure, it will be one second before it can be used again. Each subsequent failure doubles the wait time until `processor.maxPenality` is reached.

Summary

In this chapter we covered in depth the HDFS sink, the Flume output that writes streaming data into the HDFS. We covered how Flume can separate data into different HDFS paths based on time or contents of Flume headers. Several file-rolling techniques were also discussed including the following:

- Time rotation
- Event count rotation
- Size rotation
- Rotation on idle only

Compression was discussed as a means to reduce storage requirements in HDFS and should be used when possible. Besides storage savings, it is often faster to read a compressed file and decompress in memory than it is to read an uncompressed file. This will result in performance improvements in MapReduce jobs run on this data. Splitability of compressed data was also covered as a factor in deciding which compression algorithm to use.

Event serializers were introduced as the mechanism by which Flume events are converted into an external storage format including the following:

- Text (body only)
- Text and Headers (headers and body)
- Avro Serialization (with optional compression)

Next, various file formats including the following:

- Sequence Files (Hadoop key/value files)
- Data Streams (uncompressed data files, such as Avro containers)
- Compressed data streams

Finally, we covered sink groups as a means of routing events to different sources using load balancing or failover paths that can be used to eliminate single points of failure in routing data to its destination.

In the next chapter, we will discuss various input mechanisms (Sources) that will feed your configured channels covered back in *Chapter 3, Channels*.

5
Sources and Channel Selectors

Now that we have covered channels and sinks, we will cover some of the more common ways to get data into your Flume agents. As discussed in *Chapter 1, Overview and Architecture*, the source is the input point into the Flume agent. There are many sources available with the Flume distribution as well as many open source options available. Like most open source software, if you can't find what you need you can always write your own software by extending the `org.apache.flume.source.AbstractSource` class. Since the primary focus of this book is ingesting files of logs into Hadoop, we'll cover a few of the more appropriate sources to accomplish this.

The problem with using tail

If you had used any of the Flume 0.9 releases, you'll notice that the TailSource is no longer part of Flume. TailSource provided a mechanism to `tail` (`http://en.wikipedia.org/wiki/Tail_(Unix)`) any file on the system and create Flume events for each line of the file. Many have already used the filesystem as a handoff point between the application creating the data (for instance, `log4j`) and the mechanism responsible for moving those files someplace else (for instance, `syslog`). So, TailSource was the perfect replacement for the syslog transport without needing to make changes to the application creating the data.

As is the case with both channels and sinks, events are added and removed from a channel as part of a transaction. When you are tailing a file, there is no way to participate properly in a transaction. If a failure to write successfully to a channel occurred or if the channel was simply full (a more likely event than failure), the data couldn't be "put back" as the rollback semantics dictate.

Furthermore, if the rate of data written to a file exceeded the rate Flume could read the data, it is possible to lose one or more logfiles of input outright. For example, say you were tailing `/var/log/app.log`. When that file reaches a certain size, that file is rotated/renamed to `/var/log/app.log.1` and a new file is started `/var/log/app.log`. Let's say you had a favorable review in the press and your application logs are much higher than usual. Flume may still be reading from the rotated file (`/var/log/app.log.1`) when another rotation occurs moving `/var/log/app.log` to `/var/log/app.log.1`. The file Flume is reading is now renamed to `/var/log/app.log.2`. When Flume finishes with this file, it will move to what it thinks is the next file, `/var/log/app.log`, thus skipping the file that now resides at `/var/log/app.log.1`. This kind of data loss would go completely unnoticed and is something we want to avoid if possible.

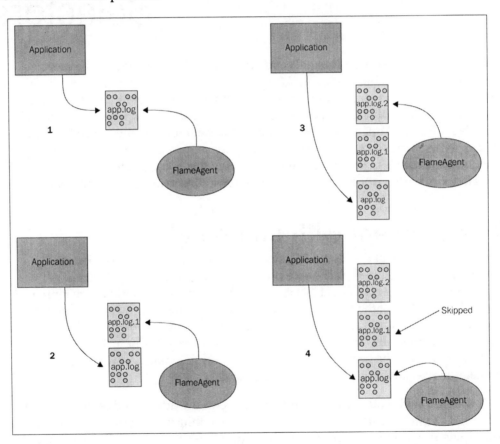

For these reasons, it was decided to remove the `tail` functionality from Flume when it was refactored. There are some workarounds for TailSource having been removed, but it should be noted that no workaround can eliminate the possibility of data loss under load under these conditions.

The exec source

The exec source provides a mechanism to run a command outside of Flume and then turn the output into Flume events. To use the exec source, set the `type` property to `exec`:

```
agent.sources.s1.type=exec
```

All sources in Flume are required to specify the list of channels to write events to using the `channels` (plural) property. This is a space-separated list of one or more channel names:

```
agent.sources.s1.channels=c1
```

The only other required parameter is the `command` property, which tells Flume what command to pass to the operating system. For instance:

```
agent.sources=s1
agent.sources.s1.channels=c1
agent.sources.s1.type=exec
agent.sources.s1.command=tail -F /var/log/app.log
```

Here I have configured a single source `s1` for an agent named `agent`. The source, an exec source, will tail the `/var/log/app.log` file and follow any rotations outside applications may perform on that logfile. All events are written to the `c1` channel. This is an example of one of the workarounds for the lack of TailSource in Flume 1.x.

Should you use the `tail -F` command in conjunction with the exec source, it is probable that the forked process will not shut down 100 percent of the time when the Flume agent shuts down or restarts. This will leave orphaned tail processes that will never exit. `tail -F` by definition has no end. Even if you delete the file being tailed (at least in Linux), the running tail process will keep the file handle open indefinitely. This keeps the file's space from actually being reclaimed until the tail process exits — which it won't. I think you are beginning to see why the Flume developers don't like tailing files.

If you go down this route, be sure to periodically scan the process tables for `tail -F` whose parent PID is 1. These are effectively dead processes and need to be killed manually.

Here is a list of the other properties you can use with the exec source:

Key	Required	Type	Default
type	Yes	String	exec
channels	Yes	String	Space-separated list of channels
command	Yes	String	
restart	No	boolean	false
restartThrottle	No	long (milliseconds)	10000 milliseconds
logStdErr	No	boolean	false
batchSize	No	int	20

Not every command keeps running, either because it fails (like when the channel it is writing to is full) or the command is designed to exit immediately. In this example, we want to record the system load via the Linux uptime command, which prints out some system information to stdout and exits:

```
agent.sources.s1.command=uptime
```

This command will immediately exit, so you can use the restart and restartThrottle properties to run it periodically:

```
agent.sources.s1.command=uptime
agent.sources.s1.restart=true
agent.sources.s1.restartThrottle=60000
```

This will produce one event per minute. In the tail example, should the channel fill causing the exec source to fail, you can use these properties to restart the exec source. In this case, setting the restart property will start the tailing of the file from the beginning of the current file, thus producing duplicates. Depending on how long the restartThrottle value is set to, you may have missed some data due to a file rotation outside of Flume. Furthermore, the channel may *still* be unable to accept data, in which case the source will fail again. Setting this value too low means giving less time to the channel to drain and unlike some of the sinks we saw, there is not an option for exponential backoff.

Sometimes commands write the output you want to capture to StdErr. If you want these lines included as well, set the logStdErr property to true. There isn't a property to turn *off* the StdOut lines as input (but you can filter them out when we get to discussing interceptors in *Chapter 6, Interceptors, ETL, and Routing*).

Finally, you can specify the number of events to write per transaction by changing the batchSize property. You may need to set this value higher than the default of 20, if your input data is large and you find that you cannot write to your channel fast enough. Using a higher batch size reduces the overall average transaction overhead per event. Testing with different values and monitoring the channel's put rate is the only way to know for sure.

The spooling directory source

In an effort to avoid all the assumptions inherent in tailing a file, a new source was devised to keep track of which files have been converted into Flume events and which still need to be processed. The spooling directory source is given a directory to watch for new files to appear. It is assumed that files copied to this directory are complete; otherwise, the source might try and send a partial file. It also assumes that filenames never change; otherwise, the source would loose its place on restarts as to which files have been sent and which have not. The filename condition can be met in log4j by using the DailyRollingFileAppender rather than the RollingFileAppender, however, the currently open file would need to be written into one directory and copied to the spool directory after being closed. None of the log4j appenders shipping have this capability.

That said, if you are using the Linux logrotate program in your environment, this might be of interest. You can move completed files to a separate directory using a postrotate script.

Remember, you will need a separate process to clean out any old files in the spool directory after they have been marked sent by Flume or your disk will eventually fill up.

To create a spooling directory source, set the type property to spooldir. You must set the directory to watch the spoolDir property:

```
agent.sources=s1
agent.sources.channels=c1
agent.sources.s1.type=spooldir
agent.sources.s1.spoolDir=/path/to/files
```

Here is a summary of the properties for the spooling directory source:

Key	Required	Type	Default
type	Yes	String	spooldir
channels	Yes	String	Space-separated list of channels
spoolDir	Yes	String	Path to directory to spool
fileSuffix	No	String	.COMPLETED
fileHeader	No	boolean	false
fileHeaderKey	No	String	file
batchSize	No	int	10
bufferMaxLines	No	int	100
maxBufferLineLength	No	int	5000

When a file has been transmitted completely it will be renamed with a .COMPLETED extension unless overridden by setting the fileSuffix property. For example:

```
agent.source.s1.fileSuffix=.DONE
```

If you want the absolute file path attached to each event, set the fileHeader property to true. This will create a header with the file key unless set to something else using the fileHeaderKey property. For example:

```
agent.source.s1.fileHeader=true
agent.source.s1.fileHeaderKey=sourceFile
```

This would add the header {sourceFile=/path/to/files/foo.1234.log} if the event was read from the /path/to/files/foo.1234.log file.

The batchSize property allows you to tune the number of events per transaction for writes to the channel. Increasing this may provide better throughput at the cost of larger transactions (and possibly larger rollbacks). The bufferMaxLines property is used to set the size of the memory buffer used in reading files by multiplying it with maxBufferLineLength. If your data is very short, you might consider increasing bufferMaxLines while reducing maxBufferLineLength. In this case, it will result in better throughput without increasing your memory overhead. That said, if you have events longer than 5000 characters, you'll want to set maxBufferLineLength higher.

Finally, you'll want to make sure that whatever mechanism is writing new files into your spooling directory creates unique filenames, such as adding a timestamp (and possibly more). Reusing a filename will confuse the source and your data may not be processed.

As always, remember that restarts and errors will create duplicate events on any files in the spooling directory that are retransmitted due to not being marked as finished.

Syslog sources

Syslog has been around for decades and is often used as an operating system level mechanism for capturing and moving logs around systems. In many ways there are overlaps with some of the functionality that Flume provides. There is even a Hadoop module for **rsyslog**, one of the more modern variants of syslog (http://www.rsyslog.com/doc/rsyslog_conf_modules.html/omhdfs.html). Generally, I don't like solutions that couple technologies that may version independently. If you use this rsyslog/Hadoop integration, you would be required to update the version of Hadoop you compiled into rsyslog at the same time you upgraded your Hadoop cluster to a new major version. This may be logistically difficult if you have a large number of servers and/or environments. Backward compatibility in Hadoop wire protocols is something that is being actively worked on in the Hadoop community, but currently isn't the norm. We'll talk more about this in *Chapter 7, Monitoring Flume*, when we discuss tiering data flows.

Syslog has an older UDP transport as well as a newer TCP protocol that can handle data larger than a single UDP packet can transmit (about 64k), as well as deal with network-related congestion events that might require the data to be retransmitted.

Finally, there are some undocumented properties on the syslog sources that allow for adding additional regular expression matching patterns for messages that do not conform to the RFC standards. I won't be discussing these additional settings, but you should be aware of them if you run into frequent parsing errors. In this case, have a look at the source for org.apache.flume.source.SyslogUtils for implementation details to find the cause.

More details on syslog terms (like what a facility is) and standard formats can be found in **RFC 3164** (http://tools.ietf.org/html/rfc3164) and **RFC 5424** (http://tools.ietf.org/html/rfc5424).

The syslog UDP source

The UDP version of syslog is usually safe to use when you are receiving data from the server's local syslog process, provided the data is small enough (less than around 64k).

> The implementation for this source has chosen 2500 bytes as the maximum payload size regardless of what your network can actually handle. So, if your payload will be larger than this, use one of the TCP sources instead.

To create a syslog UDP source, set the `type` property to `syslogudp`. You must set the port to listen on using the `port` property. The optional `host` property specifies the bind address. If no host is specified, all IPs for the server will be used—the same as specifying `0.0.0.0`. In this example, we will only listen for local UDP connections on port 5140:

```
agent.sources=s1
agent.sources.channels=c1
agent.sources.s1.type=syslogudp
agent.sources.s1.host=localhost
agent.sources.s1.port=5140
```

If you want syslog to forward a tailed file, you could add a line such as the following to your syslog configuration file:

```
*.err;*.alert;*.crit;*.emerg;kern.*       @localhost:5140
```

This would send all error, alert, critical, emergency priority, and kernel messages of any priority into your Flume source. The single @ symbol designates that the UDP protocol should be used.

Here is a summary of properties for the syslog UDP source:

Key	Required	Type	Default
type	Yes	String	syslogudp
channels	Yes	String	Space-separated list of channels
port	Yes	int	
host	No	String	0.0.0.0

The Flume headers created by the syslog UDP source are summarized as follows:

Header key	Description
Facility	The syslog facility. See the syslog documentation.
Priority	The syslog priority. See the syslog documentation.
timestamp	The time of the syslog event translated into an epoch timestamp. Omitted if not parsed from one of the standard RFC formats.
hostname	The parsed hostname in the syslog message. Omitted if not parsed.
flume.syslog. status	There was a problem parsing the syslog message's headers. Set to `Invalid` if the payload didn't conform to the RFCs. Set to `Incomplete` if the message was longer than the `eventSize` value (for UDP this is set internally to 2500 bytes). Omitted if everything is fine.

The syslog TCP source

As previously mentioned, the syslog TCP source provides an endpoint for messages over TCP, allowing for a larger payload size and TCP retry semantics that should be used for any reliable inter-server communications.

To create a syslog TCP source, set the `type` property to `syslogtcp`. You must still set the bind address and port to listen on:

```
agent.sources=s1
agent.sources.s1.type=syslogtcp
agent.sources.s1.host=0.0.0.0
agent.sources.s1.port=12345
```

If your syslog implementation supports syslog over TCP, the configuration is usually the same except a double @ symbol is used to indicated TCP transport. Here is the same example using TCP where I am forwarding to a Flume agent that is running on a different server named `flume-1`:

```
*.err;*.alert;*.crit;*.emerg;kern.*        @@flume-1:12345
```

There are some optional properties for the syslog TCP source:

Key	Required	Type	Default
type	Yes	String	syslogtcp
channels	Yes	String	Space-separated list of channels
port	Yes	int	
host	No	String	0.0.0.0
eventSize	No	int (bytes)	2500 bytes

The Flume headers created by the syslog TCP source are summarized as follows:

Header key	Description
Facility	The syslog facility. See the syslog documentation.
Priority	The syslog priority. See the syslog documentation.
timestamp	The time of the syslog event translated into an epoch timestamp. Omitted if not parsed from one of the standard RFC formats.
hostname	The parsed hostname in the syslog message. Omitted if not parsed.
flume.syslog. status	There was a problem parsing the syslog message's headers. Set to `Invalid` if the payload didn't conform to the RFCs. Set to `Incomplete` if the message was longer than the configured `eventSize`. Omitted if everything is fine.

The multiport syslog TCP source

The multiport syslog TCP source is nearly identical in functionality to the syslog TCP source, except that it can listen on multiple ports for input. You may need to use this capability should you be unable to change which port syslog will use in its forwarding rules (it may not be your server at all). More likely you will use this to read multiple formats using one source to write into different channels. We'll cover that in a moment in the *Channel selectors* section.

To configure this source, set the `type` property to `multiport_syslogtcp`:

```
agent.sources.s1.type=multiport_syslogtcp
```

Like the other syslog sources, you need to specify the port, but in this case it is a space-separated list of ports. You can use this only if you have one port specified. The property for this is `ports` (plural):

```
agent.sources.s1.type=multiport_syslogtcp
agent.sources.s1.channels=c1
agent.sources.s1.ports=33333 44444
agent.sources.s1.host=0.0.0.0
```

This configures the multiport syslog TCP source named `s1` to listen for any incoming connections on ports `33333` and `44444` and send them to channel `c1`.

In order to tell which event came from which port, you can set the optional `portHeader` property to the name of the key whose value will be the port number. If I added this property to the configuration:

```
agent.sources.s1.portHeader=port
```

Then any events received from port `33333`, would have a header key/value of `{"port"="33333"}`. As you saw in *Chapter 4, Sinks and Sink Processors*, you can now use this value (any header really) as part of your HDFS sink file path convention like so:

```
agent.sinks.k1.hdfs.path=/logs/%{hostname}/%{port}/%Y/%m/%D/%H
```

Here is a complete table of the properties:

Key	Required	Type	Default
type	Yes	String	syslogtcp
channels	Yes	String	Space-separated list of channels
ports	Yes	int	Space-separated list of port numbers

Key	Required	Type	Default
host	No	String	0.0.0.0
eventSize	No	int (bytes)	2500 bytes
portHeader	No	String	
batchSize	No	int	100
readBufferSize	No	int (bytes)	1024
numProcessors	No	int	Automatically detected
charset.default	No	String	UTF-8
charset.port.PORT#	No	String	

This TCP source has some additional tunable options over the standard TCP syslog source, which you may want to tune. The first is the batchSize property. This is the number of events processed per transaction with the channel. There is also the readBufferSize property that specifies the internal buffer size used by an internal Mina library. Finally, the numProcessors property is used to size the worker thread pool in Mina. Before you tune these parameters, you may want to familiarize yourself with Mina (http://mina.apache.org/) and look at the source code before deviating from the defaults.

Finally, you can specify a default and per-port character encoding to use when converting between strings and byte[]s.

```
agent.sources.s1.charset.default=UTF-16
agent.sources.s1.charset.port.33333=UTF-8
```

This sample configuration shows that all ports would be interpreted using UTF-16 encoding except for port 33333 traffic, which would use UTF-8.

The Flume headers created by this source are summarized here:

Header key	Description
Facility	The syslog facility. See the syslog documentation.
Priority	The syslog priority. See the syslog documentation.
timestamp	The time of the syslog event translated into an epoch timestamp. Omitted if not parsed from one of the standard RFC formats.
hostname	The parsed hostname in the syslog message. Omitted if not parsed.
flume.syslog.status	There was a problem parsing the syslog message's headers. Set to Invalid if the payload didn't conform to the RFCs. Set to Incomplete if the message was longer than the configured eventSize. Omitted if everything is fine.

Channel selectors

As we previously discussed in *Chapter 1, Overview and Architecture*, a source can write to one or more channels. This is why the property is plural (`channels` instead of `channel`). There are two ways multiple channels can be handled. The event can be written to all of the channels or to just one based on some Flume header value. The internal mechanism for this in Flume is called a **channel selector**.

The selector for any channel can be specified using the `selector.type` property. Any selector specific properties begin with the usual source prefix; agent name, the keyword sources, and the source name:

```
agent.sources.s1.selector.type=replicating
```

Replicating

By default, if you do not specify a selector for a source, `replicating` is the default. The replicating selector writes the same event to all channels in the source's channels list:

```
agent.sources.s1.channels=c1 c2 c3
agent.sources.s1.selector.type=replicating
```

In this example, every event will be written to all three channels, c1, c2, and c3.

There is an optional property on this selector called `optional`. It is a space-separated list of channels that are optional. That is, if I set the following:

```
agent.sources.s1.channels=c1 c2 c3
agent.sources.s1.selector.type=replicating
agent.sources.s1.selector.optional=c2 c3
```

Any failures to write to channels c2 or c3 would not fail the transaction and any data written to c1 would be committed. In the previous example with no optional channels, any single channel failure would roll back the transaction for them all.

Multiplexing

If you wanted to send different events to different channels, you would use a multiplexing channel selector by setting `selector.type` to `multiplexing`. You also need to tell the channel selector which header to use by setting the `selector.header` property.

```
agent.sources.s1.selector.type=multiplexing
agent.sources.s1.selector.header=port
```

Let's assume we used the multiport syslog TCP source to listen on four ports, 11111, 22222, 33333, and 44444 with a `portHeader` setting of `port`. Consider this configuration:

```
agent.sources.s1.selector.default=c2
agent.sources.s1.selector.mapping.11111=c1 c2
agent.sources.s1.selector.mapping.44444=c2
agent.sources.s1.selector.optional.44444=c3
```

This would result in port 22222 and port 33333 traffic going to channel c2 only. The traffic from port 11111 would go to channels c1 and c2. A failure on either channel would result in nothing being added to either channel. The traffic from port 44444 would go to channels c2 and c3; however, a failure to write to c3 would still commit the transaction to channel c2 (and c3 would not be attempted again with that event).

Summary

In this chapter we covered in depth the various sources which you can use to ingest log data into Flume, including the following:

- The exec source
- Syslog sources (UDP, TCP, and multiport TCP)

We discussed replicating the old TailSource functionality in Flume 0.9 and the problems using tail semantics in general.

We also covered channel selectors and how to send events to one of more channels. Specifically:

- The replicating channel selector
- The multiplexing channel selector

Optional channels were also discussed as a way to only fail a Channel put transaction for only some of the Channels when more than one is used.

In the next chapter, we'll introduce Interceptors that will allow in-flight inspection and transformation of Events. Used in conjunction with Channel Selectors, Interceptors provide the final piece to creating complex data flows with Flume.

6
Interceptors, ETL, and Routing

The final piece of functionality necessary in your data processing pipeline is the ability to inspect and transform events in flight. This can be accomplished using interceptors. **Interceptors**, as we discussed in *Chapter 1, Overview and Architecture*, can be inserted after a source or before a sink.

Interceptors

An interceptor's functionality can be summed up by this method:

```
public Event intercept(Event event);
```

It is passed as a Flume **event** and it returns as a Flume **event**. It may do nothing; that is, the same unaltered event is returned. Often, it alters the event in some useful way. If null is returned, the event is dropped.

To add interceptors to a source, simply add the interceptors property to the named source. For example:

```
agent.sources.s1.interceptors=i1 i2 i3
```

This defines three interceptors, i1, i2, and i3, on the s1 source for the agent named agent.

 Interceptors are run in the order they are listed. In the preceding example, i2 will receive the output from i1. i3 will receive the output from i2. Finally, the channel selector receives the output from i3.

Now that we have defined the interceptor by name, we need to specify its type as follows:

```
agent.sources.s1.interceptors.i1.type=TYPE1
agent.sources.s1.interceptors.i1.additionalProperty1=VALUE
agent.sources.s1.interceptors.i2.type=TYPE2
agent.sources.s1.interceptors.i3.type=TYPE3
```

Let's look at some of the interceptors that, come bundled with Flume, to get a better idea of how to configure them.

Timestamp

The Timestamp interceptor, as its name suggests, adds a header with the `timestamp` key to the Flume event if one doesn't already exist. To use it, set the `type` property to `timestamp`.

If the event already contains a timestamp header, it will be overwritten with the current time unless configured to preserve the original value by setting the `preserveExisting` property to `true`.

Here is a table summarizing the properties for the timestamp interceptor:

Key	Required	Type	Default
type	Yes	String	timestamp
preserveExisting	No	Boolean	false

Here is what a total configuration might look like for a source if we only want it to add a timestamp header if none exists:

```
agent.sources.s1.interceptors=i1
agent.sources.s1.interceptors.i1.type=timestamp
agent.sources.s1.interceptors.i1.preserveExisting=true
```

Recall this HDFSSink path from *Chapter 4, Sinks and Sink Processors*, utilizing the event date:

```
agent.sinks.k1.hdfs.path=/logs/apache/%Y/%m/%D/%H
```

The `timestamp` header is what determines this path. If it is missing, you can be sure Flume will not know where to create the files and you will not get the result you are looking for.

Host

Similar in simplicity to the Timestamp interceptor, the Host interceptor will add a header to the event containing the IP address of the current Flume agent. To use it, set the `type` property to `host`.

```
agent.sources.s1.interceptors=i1
agent.sources.s1.interceptors.type=host
```

The key for this header will be `host` unless you specify something else using the `hostHeader` property. Like before, an existing header will be overwritten, unless you set the `preserveExisting` property to `true`. Finally, if you want a reverse DNS lookup of the hostname to be used instead of IP as a value, set the `useIP` property to `false`. Remember that reverse lookups will add processing time to your data flow.

Here is a table summarizing the properties for the Host interceptor:

Key	Required	Type	Default
type	Yes	String	host
hostHeader	No	String	host
preserveExisting	No	Boolean	false
useIP	No	Boolean	true

Here is what a total configuration might look like for a source if we only want it to add a `relayHost` header containing the DNS hostname of this agent to every event:

```
agent.sources.s1.interceptors=i1
agent.sources.s1.interceptors.i1.type=host
agent.sources.s1.interceptors.i1.hostHeader=relayHost
agent.sources.s1.interceptors.i1.useIP=false
```

This interceptor might be useful if you wanted to record the path your events took though your data flow, for instance. Chances are you are more interested in the origin of the event rather than the path it took, which is why I have yet to use this.

Static

The Static interceptor is used to insert any single key/value header into each Flume event processed. If more than one key/value is desired, you simply add additional Static interceptors. Unlike the interceptors we've looked at so far, the default behavior is to preserve existing headers with the same key. As always, my recommendation is to always specify what you want and not rely on the defaults.

I do not know why the key and value properties are not required since the defaults are not terribly useful.

Here is a table summarizing the properties for the Static interceptor:

Key	Required	Type	Default
type	Yes	String	static
key	No	String	key
value	No	String	value
preserveExisting	No	Boolean	true

Finally, let's look at an example configuration that inserts two new headers provided they don't already exist in the event:

```
agent.sources.s1.interceptors=pos env
agent.sources.s1.interceptors.pos.type=static
agent.sources.s1.interceptors.pos.key=pointOfSale
agent.sources.s1.interceptors.pos.value=US
agent.sources.s1.interceptors.env.type=static
agent.sources.s1.interceptors.env.key=environment
agent.sources.s1.interceptors.env.value=staging
```

Regular expression filtering

If you want to filter events based on the contents of the body, the regular expression filtering interceptor is your friend. Based on a regular expression you provide, it will either filter out the matched events or keep only the matching events. Start by setting the interceptor's type property to regex_filter. The pattern you want to match is specified using Java-style regular expression syntax. See these javadocs for usage details:

http://docs.oracle.com/javase/6/docs/api/java/util/regex/Pattern.html.

The pattern string is set in the regex property. Finally, you need to tell the interceptor if you want to exclude matching records by setting the excludeEvents property to true. The default (false) indicates you want to only keep events matching the pattern.

Here is a table summarizing the properties for the regular expression filtering interceptor:

Key	Required	Type	Default
type	Yes	String	regex_filter
regex	No	String	.*
excludeEvents	No	Boolean	false

In this example, any events containing the string `NullPointerException` will be dropped:

```
agent.sources.s1.interceptors=npe
agent.sources.s1.interceptors.npe.type=regex_filter
agent.sources.s1.interceptors.npe.regex=NullPointerException
agent.sources.s1.interceptors.npe.excludeEvents=true
```

Regular expression extractor

Sometimes you'll want to extract bits of your event body into Flume headers so you can perform routing via channel selectors. You can use the regular expression extractor interceptor to perform this function. Start by setting the interceptor `type` to `regex_extractor`.

```
agent.sources.s1.interceptors=e1
agent.sources.s1.interceptors.e1.type=regex_extractor
```

Like the regular expression filtering interceptor, the regular expression extractor uses the Java-style regular expression syntax. In order to extract one or more fields, you start by specifying the `regex` property with group matching parentheses. Let's assume we are looking for error numbers in our events in the form "Error: N", where N is some number:

```
agent.sources.s1.interceptors=e1
agent.sources.s1.interceptors.e1.type=regex_extractor
agent.sources.s1.interceptors.e1.regex=Error:\\s(\\d+)
```

As you can see I put capture parentheses around the number, which may comprise one or more digits. Now that I've matched my desired pattern, I need to tell Flume what to do with my match. Here we need to introduce **serializers**, which provide a pluggable mechanism for how to interpret each match. In this example I've only got one match so my space-separated list of serializer names has only one entry:

```
agent.sources.s1.interceptors=e1
agent.sources.s1.interceptors.e1.type=regex_extractor
agent.sources.s1.interceptors.e1.regex=Error:\\s(\\d+)
agent.sources.s1.interceptors.e1.serializers=ser1
agent.sources.s1.interceptors.e1.serializers.ser1.type=default
agent.sources.s1.interceptors.e1.serializers.ser1.name=error_no
```

The `name` property specifies the event key to use where the value is the matching text from the regular expression. The type of `default` (also the default if not specified) is a simple pass-through serializer. For the following event body:

```
NullPointerException: A problem occurred. Error: 123. TxnID: 5X2T9E.
```

The following header would be added to the event:

```
{ "error_no":"123" }
```

If I wanted to add the `TxnID` value as a header, I simply add another matching pattern group and serializer:

```
agent.sources.s1.interceptors=e1
agent.sources.s1.interceptors.e1.type=regex_extractor
agent.sources.s1.interceptors.e1.regex=Error:\\s(\\d+).*TxnID:\\s(\\w+)
agent.sources.s1.interceptors.e1.serializers=ser1 ser2
agent.sources.s1.interceptors.e1.serializers.ser1.type=default
agent.sources.s1.interceptors.e1.serializers.ser1.name=error_no
agent.sources.s1.interceptors.e1.serializers.ser2.type=default
agent.sources.s1.interceptors.e1.serializers.ser2.name=txnid
```

This would create the following headers for the aforementioned input:

```
{ "error_no":"123", "txnid":"5x2T9E" }
```

However, if the fields were reversed, like so:

```
NullPointerException: A problem occurred. TxnID: 5X2T9E. Error: 123.
```

I would wind up with only a header for `TxnID`. A better way to handle this kind of ordering would be to use multiple interceptors so the order didn't matter:

```
agent.sources.s1.interceptors=e1 e2
agent.sources.s1.interceptors.e1.type=regex_extractor
agent.sources.s1.interceptors.e1.regex=Error:\\s(\\d+)
agent.sources.s1.interceptors.e1.serializers=ser1
agent.sources.s1.interceptors.e1.serializers.ser1.type=default
agent.sources.s1.interceptors.e1.serializers.ser1.name=error_no
agent.sources.s1.interceptors.e2.type=regex_extractor
agent.sources.s1.interceptors.e2.regex=TxnID:\\s(\\w+)
agent.sources.s1.interceptors.e2.serializers=ser1
agent.sources.s1.interceptors.e2.serializers.ser1.type=default
agent.sources.s1.interceptors.e2.serializers.ser1.name=txnid
```

The only other type of serializer implementation that ships with Flume, other than the pass-through, is to specify the fully qualified class name of `org.apache.flume.interceptor.RegexExtractorInterceptorMillisSerializer`. This serializer is used to convert times back into milliseconds. You need to specify a pattern property based on the `org.joda.time.format.DateTimeFormat` patterns.

For instance, let's say you were ingesting Apache Web Server access logs. For example:

```
192.168.1.42 - - [29/Mar/2013:15:27:09 -0600] "GET /index.html
HTTP/1.1" 200 1037
```

The complete regular expression for this might look like this (in the form of a Java String, with backslash and quotes escaped with an extra backslash):

```
^([\\d.]+) \\S+ \\S+ \\[([\\w:/]+\\s[+\\-]\\d{4})\\] \"(.+?)\"
(\\d{3}) (\\d+)
```

The time pattern matched corresponds to the `org.joda.time.format.DateTimeFormat` pattern:

```
yyyy/MMM/dd:HH:mm:ss Z
```

This makes our configuration something like the following code:

```
agent.sources.s1.interceptors=e1
agent.sources.s1.interceptors.e1.type=regex_extractor
agent.sources.s1.interceptors.e1.regex=^([\\d.]+) \\S+ \\S+ \\
[([\\w:/]+\\s[+\\-]\\d{4})\\] \"(.+?)\" (\\d{3}) (\\d+)
agent.sources.s1.interceptors.e1.serializers=ip dt url sc bc
agent.sources.s1.interceptors.e1.serializers.ip.name=ip_address
agent.sources.s1.interceptors.e1.serializers.dt.type=org.apache.flume.
interceptor.RegexExtractorInterceptorMillisSerializer
agent.sources.s1.interceptors.e1.serializers.dt.pattern=yyyy/MMM/
dd:HH:mm:ss Z
agent.sources.s1.interceptors.e1.serializers.dt.name=timestamp
agent.sources.s1.interceptors.e1.serializers.url.name=http_request
agent.sources.s1.interceptors.e1.serializers.sc.name=status_code
agent.sources.s1.interceptors.e1.serializers.bc.name=bytes_xfered
```

This would create the following headers for the aforementioned sample:

```
{ "ip_address":"192.168.1.42", "timestamp":"1364588829",
"http_request":"GET /index.html HTTP/1.1", "status_code":"200",
"bytes_xfered":"1037" }
```

The body content is unaffected. You'll also notice I didn't specify `default` for the type of the other serializers as that is the default.

 There is no overwrite checking in this interceptor type. For instance, using the `timestamp` key will overwrite the event's previous time value, if there was one.

You can implement your own serializers for this interceptor by implementing the `org.apache.flume.interceptor.RegexExtractorInterceptorSerializer` interface. However, if your goal is to move data from the body of an event to the header, you'll probably want to implement a custom interceptor so that you can alter the body contents in addition to setting the header value, otherwise the data will be effectively duplicated.

To summarize let's review the properties for this interceptor:

Key	Required	Type	Default
`type`	Yes	String	regex_extractor
`regex`	Yes	String	
`serializers`	Yes	Space-separated list of serializer names	
`serializers.NAME.name`	Yes	String	
`serializers.NAME.type`	No	Default or FQDN of implementation	`default`
`serializers.NAME.PROP`	No	Serializer-specific properties	

Custom interceptors

If there is one piece of custom code you will add to your Flume implementation, it will most likely be a custom interceptor. As mentioned earlier, you implement the `org.apache.flume.interceptor.Interceptor` interface and the associated `org.apache.flume.interceptor.Interceptor.Builder` interface.

Let's say I needed to URL-decode my event body. The code would look something as follows:

```
public class URLDecode implements Interceptor {


  public void initialize() {}

  public Event intercept(Event event) {
    try {
      byte[] decoded = URLDecoder.decode(new String(event.getBody()),
"UTF-8").getBytes("UTF-8");
      event.setBody(decoded);
    } catch UnsupportedEncodingException e) {
      // This shouldn't happen. Fall through to unaltered event.
    }
```

```
      return event;
    }

    public List<Event> intercept(List<Event> events) {
      for (Event event:events) {
        intercept(event);
      }
      return events;
    }

    public void close() {}

    public static class Builder implements Interceptor.Builder {
      public Interceptor build() {
        return new URLDecode();
      }
      public void configure(Context context) {}
    }
  }
}
```

Then to configure my new interceptor, use the FQDN for the `Builder` class as the type:

```
agent.sources.s1.interceptors=i1
agent.sources.s1.interceptors.i1.type=com.example.URLDecoder$Builder
```

For more examples of how to pass and validate properties, look at the Flume source code at existing interceptor implementations for inspiration.

Keep in mind that any heavy processing in your custom interceptor can affect overall throughput, so be mindful of object churn or computationally intensive processing in your implementations.

Tiering data flows

In *Chapter 1, Overview and Architecture*, we talked about tiering your data flows. There are several reasons for wanting to do this. You may want to limit the number of Flume agents that directly connect to your Hadoop cluster to limit the number of parallel requests. You may also lack sufficient disk space on your application servers to store a significant amount of data while you are performing maintenance on your Hadoop cluster. Whatever your reason or use case, the most common mechanism for chaining Flume agents is using the Avro Source/Sink pair.

Avro Source/Sink

We covered Avro a bit in *Chapter 4, Sink and Sink Processors,* when we discussed using it as an on-disk serialization format for files stored in HDFS. Here we'll put it to use in communication between Flume agents. A typical configuration might look something as follows:

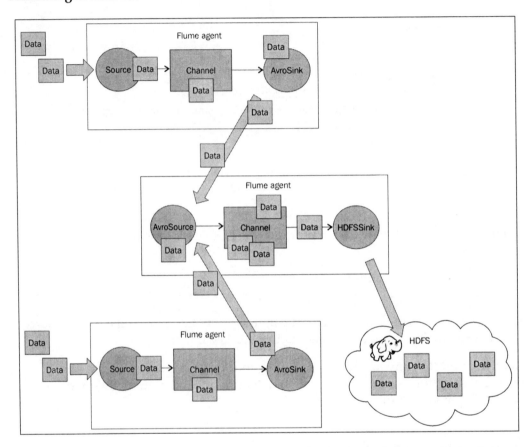

To use the Avro Source, you specify the type property with a value of avro. You need to provide a bind address and port number to listen on:

```
collector.sources=av1
collector.sources.av1.type=avro
collector.sources.av1.bind=0.0.0.0
collector.sources.av1.port=42424
collector.sources.av1.channels=ch1
collector.channels=ch1
```

```
collector.channels.ch1.type=memory
collector.sinks=k1
collector.sinks.k1.type=hdfs
collector.sinks.k1.channel=ch1
collector.sinks.k1.hdfs.path=/path/in/hdfs
```

Here we have configured the agent on the right that listens on port 42424, uses a memory channel, and writes to HDFS. Here I've used the memory channel for brevity of this example configuration. Also, note that I've given this agent a different name, collector, just to avoid confusion.

The agents on the left—feeding the collector tier—might have a configuration similar to this. I have left the sources off this configuration for brevity:

```
client.channels=ch1
client.channels.ch1.type=memory
client.sinks=k1
client.sinks.k1.type=avro
client.sinks.k1.channel=ch1
client.sinks.k1.hostname=collector.example.com
client.sinks.k1.port=42424
```

The hostname value, collector.example.com, has nothing to do with the agent name on that machine, it is the host name (or you can use an IP) of the target machine with the receiving Avro Source. This configuration, named client, would be applied to both agents on the left assuming both had similar source configurations.

Since I don't like single points of failure, I would configure two collector agents with the preceding configuration and instead set each client agent to round robin between the two using a sink group. Again, I've left off the sources for brevity:

```
client.channels=ch1
client.channels.ch1.type=memory
client.sinks=k1 k2
client.sinks.k1.type=avro
client.sinks.k1.channel=ch1
client.sinks.k1.hostname=collectorA.example.com
client.sinks.k1.port=42424
client.sinks.k2.type=avro
client.sinks.k2.channel=ch1
client.sinks.k2.hostname=collectorB.example.com
client.sinks.k2.port=42424
client.sinkgroups=g1
client.sinkgroups.g1=k1 k2
client.sinkgroups.g1.processor.type=load_balance
client.sinkgroups.g1.processor.selector=round_robin
client.sinkgroups.g1.processor.backoff=true
```

Command-line Avro

The Avro Source can also be used in conjunction with one of the command-line options you may have noticed back in *Chapter 2, Flume Quick Start*. Rather than running flume-ng with the agent parameter, you can pass the avro-client parameter to send one or more files to an Avro Source. These are the avro-client specific options from the help text:

```
avro-client options:
  --dirname <dir>        directory to stream to avro source
  --host,-H <host>       hostname to which events will be sent
(required)
  --port,-p <port>       port of the avro source (required)
  --filename,-F <file>   text file to stream to avro source [default:
std input]
  --headerFile,-R <file> headerFile containing headers as key/value
pairs on each new line
  --help,-h              display help text
```

This variation is very useful for testing, resending data manually due to errors, or importing older data stored elsewhere.

Just like an Avro Sink, you have to specify the host name and port you will be sending data to. You can send a single file with the --filename option or all the files in a directory with the --dirname option. If you specify neither of these, stdin will be used. Here is how you might send a file named foo.log into the Flume agent we previously configured:

```
$ ./flume-ng avro-client --filename foo.log --host collector.example.
com --port 42424
```

Each line of the input will be converted into a single Flume event.

Optionally, you can specify a file containing key/value pairs to set Flume header values. The file uses the Java property file syntax. If I had a file named headers.properties:

```
pointOfSale=US
environment=staging
```

Then including the --headerFile option would set these two headers on every event created:

```
$ ./flume-ng avro-client --filename foo.log --headerFile headers.
properties --host collector.example.com --port 42424
```

Log4J Appender

As we discussed in *Chapter 5, Sources and Channel Selectors*, there are issues that may arise from using a filesystem file as a source. One way to avoid this problem is to use the Flume Log4J Appender in your Java application(s). Under the hood, it uses the same Avro communication that the Avro Sink uses, so you need only configure it to send data to an Avro Source.

The Appender has two properties ,shown as follows in XML:

```
<appender name="FLUME" class="org.apache.flume.clients.log4jappender.
Log4jAppender">
  <param name="Hostname" value="collector.example.com"/>
  <param name="Port" value="42424"/>
</appender>
```

The format of the body will be dictated by the Appender's configured layout (not shown). The `log4j` fields that get mapped to Flume headers are summarized in the following table:

Flume header key	Log4J LoggingEvent field
`flume.client.log4j.logger.name`	`event.getLoggerName()`
`flume.client.log4j.log.level`	`event.getLevel()` as a number. See `org.apache.log4j.Level` for mappings.
`flume.client.log4j.timestamp`	`event.getTimeStamp()`
`flume.client.log4j.message.encoding`	N/A. Always UTF8.
`flume.client.log4j.logger.other`	Will only see this if there was a problem mapping one of the previous fields – so normally this won't be present.

See `http://logging.apache.org/log4j/1.2/` for more details on using Log4J.

You will need to include the `flume-ng-sdk` JAR in the classpath of your Java application at runtime to use Flume's Log4J Appender.

Keep in mind that if there is a problem sending data to the Avro Source, the Appender will throw an exception and the log message will be dropped since there is no place to put it. Keeping it in memory could quickly overload your JVM heap, which is usually considered worse than dropping the data record.

The Load Balancing Log4J Appender

I'm sure you noticed that the previous Log4j Appender only has a single host name/port in its configuration. If you wanted to spread the load across multiple collector agents, either for additional capacity or for fault-tolerance, you can use the `LoadBalancingLog4jAppender`. This Appender has a single required property named `Hosts`, which is a space-separated list of host names and port numbers separated by a colon like so:

```
<appender name="FLUME" class="org.apache.flume.clients.log4jappender.
LoadBalancingLog4jAppender">
   <param name="Hosts" value="server1:42424 server2:42424"/>
</appender>
```

There is an optional property, `Selector`, which specifies the method that you want to load balance. Valid values are `RANDOM` and `ROUND_ROBIN`. If not specified, the default is `RANDOM`. You can implement your own selector, but that is outside the scope of this book. If you are interested, go have a look at the well-documented source code for the `LoadBalancingLog4jAppender` class.

The default selector mechanism for the Load Balancing Log4J Appender if not specified is random. You'll notice this differs from the similar functionality of the sink group covered in *Chapter 4, Sink and Sink Processors*, where the default selector value is round robin.

This is yet another example of why you should always specify what you intend and not rely on the defaults.

Finally, there is another optional property to override the maximum time for exponential back off when a server cannot be contacted. Initially, if a server cannot be contacted, one second will need to pass before that server is tried again. Each time the server is unavailable, the retry time doubles, up to a default 30-second maximum. If we wanted to increase this maximum to 2 minutes, we could specify a `MaxBackoff` property in milliseconds like so:

```
<appender name="FLUME" class="org.apache.flume.clients.log4jappender.
LoadBalancingLog4jAppender">
   <param name="Hosts" value="server1:42424 server2:42424"/>
   <param name="Selector" value="ROUND_ROBIN"/>
   <param name="MaxBackoff" value="120000"/>
</appender>
```

In this example, we have also overridden the default random selector to use the round robin selection.

Routing

Routing of data to different destinations based on content should be fairly straightforward now that you've been introduced to all the various mechanisms in Flume.

The first step is to get the data you want to switch on into a Flume header by means of a source-side interceptor, if the header isn't already available. The second step is to use a multiplexing channel selector on that header value to switch the data to an alternate channel.

For instance, let's say you wanted to capture all the exceptions to HDFS. In this configuration you can see events coming in on the source s1 via Avro on port 42424. The event is tested to see if the body contains the text "Exception". If it does, it creates a header key exception (with the value of Exception). This header is used to switch these events to channel c1, and ultimately HDFS. If the event didn't match the pattern, it would not have the exception header and would get passed to channel c2 via the default selector, where it would be forwarded via Avro serialization to port 12345 on the server foo.example.com.

```
agent.sources=s1
agent.sources.s1.type=avro
agent.sources.s1.bind=0.0.0.0
agent.sources.s1.port=42424
agent.sources.s1.interceptors=i1
agent.sources.s1.interceptors.i1.type=regex_extractor
agent.sources.s1.interceptors.i1.regex=(Exception)
agent.sources.s1.interceptors.i1.serializers=ex
agent.sources.s1.intercetpros.i1.serializers.ex.name=exception
agent.sources.s1.selector.type=multiplexing
agent.sources.s1.selector.header=exception
agent.sources.s1.selector.mapping.Exception=c1
agent.sources.s1.selector.default=c2
agent.channels=c1 c2
agent.channels.c1.type=memory
agent.channels.c2.type=memory
agent.sinks=k1 k2
agent.sinks.k1.type=hdfs
agent.sinks.k1.channel=c1
agent.sinks.k1.hdfs.path=/logs/exceptions/%y/%M/%d/%H
agent.sinks.k2.type=avro
agent.sinks.k2.channel=c2
agent.sinks.k2.hostname=foo.example.com
agent.sinks.k2.port=12345
```

Summary

In this chapter we covered the following various interceptors shipped with Flume:

- Timestamp: This is used to add a timestamp header, possibly overwriting an existing one.

- Host: This is used to add the Flume agent host name or IP as a header in the event.

- Static: This is used to add static String headers.

- Regular expression filtering: This is used to include or exclude events based on a matched regular expression.

- Regular expression extractor: This is used to create headers from matched regular expression headers. It is also useful for routing with channel selectors.

- Custom: This is used to create any custom transformations you need that you can't find elsewhere.

We also covered tiering data flows using the Avro Source and Sink.

Next we introduced two Log4J Appenders, a single path and a load-balancing version, for direct integration with Java applications.

Finally, we gave an example of using interceptors in conjunction with a channel selector to provide routing decision logic.

In the next chapter we will cover monitoring of Flume data flows using Ganglia.

7
Monitoring Flume

The User Guide for Flume states:

> *Monitoring in Flume is still a work in progress. Changes can happen very often. Several Flume components report metrics to the JMX platform MBean server. These metrics can be queried using JConsole.*

While JMX is fine for causal browsing of metric values, the number of eyeballs looking at JConsole doesn't scale when you have hundreds or even thousands of servers sending data all over the place. What you need is a way to watch everything all at once. But what are the important things to look for? That is a very difficult question, but I'll try and cover several of the items I feel are important as we cover monitoring options in this chapter.

Monitoring the agent process

The most obvious type of monitoring you'll want to perform is the Flume agent process monitoring, that is, making sure the agent is still running. There are many products that do this kind of process monitoring, so there is no way we can cover them all. If you work at a company of any reasonable size, chances are there is already a system in place for this. If this is the case, do not go off and build your own. The last thing operations wants is yet another screen to watch 24/7.

Monit

If you do not already have something in place, one freemium option is **Monit** (http://mmonit.com/monit/). The developers of Monit have a paid version that provides more bells and whistles you may want to consider. Even in the free form, it can provide you a way to check that the Flume agent is running, restart it if it isn't, and send you an e-mail when this happens so you can look into why it died.

Monit does much more, but this functionality is what we will cover here. If you are smart, and I know you are, you will add checks on the disk, CPU, and memory usage at a minimum, in addition to what we cover in this chapter.

Nagios

Another option for Flume agent process monitoring is **Nagios** (`http://www.nagios.org/`). Like Monit, you can configure Nagios to watch your Flume agents and alert you via WebUI, e-mail, or an SNMP trap. That said, it doesn't have restart capabilities. The community is quite strong and there are many plugins for other applications available. My company uses this to check the availability of Hadoop Web UIs. While not a complete picture of health, it does provide more information to the overall monitoring of our Hadoop ecosystem.

Again, if you already have tools in place at your company, see if you can re-use them before bringing in another tool.

Monitoring performance metrics

Now that we have covered a few options for process monitoring, how do you know if your application is actually doing the work you think it is? On many occasions I've seen a stuck `syslog-ng` process that appeared to be running, but it just wasn't sending any data. I'm not picking on `syslog-ng` specifically; all software does this when conditions occur that it isn't designed to deal with.

When talking about Flume data flows, you need to monitor the following:

- Data entering sources is within expected rates
- Data isn't overflowing your channels
- Data is exiting sinks at an expected rates

Flume has a pluggable monitoring framework, but as mentioned at the beginning of the chapter, it is still very much a work in progress. That doesn't mean you shouldn't use it since that would be foolish. It means you'll want to prepare extra testing and integration time whenever you upgrade.

While not covered in the Flume documentation, it is common to enable JMX in your Flume JVM (`http://bit.ly/javajmx`) and use the Nagios JMX plugin (`http://bit.ly/nagiosjmx`) to alert on performance abnormalities in your Flume agents.

Ganglia

One of the available monitoring options for watching Flume internal metrics is **Ganglia integration**. Ganglia (`http://ganglia.sourceforge.net/`) is an open source monitoring tool used to collect metrics, display graphs, and can be tiered to handle very large installations. To send your Flume metrics to your Ganglia cluster, you need to pass some properties at startup time to your agent:

Java property	Value	Description
`flume.monitoring.type`	`gangla`	Set to `gangla`.
`flume.monitoring.hosts`	`host1:port1,host2:port2`	A comma-separated list of host:port pairs for your gmond process(es).
`flume.monitoring.pollInterval`	`60`	The number of seconds between sending of data (default: 60 seconds).
`flume.monitoring.isGanglia3`	`false`	Set to `true` if using older ganglia 3 protocol. Default is to send using v3.1 protocol.

Look at each instance of gmond within the same network broadcast domain (since reachability is based on multicast packets), and find the `udp_recv_channel` block in `gmond.conf`. Let's say I had two nearby servers with these two corresponding configuration blocks:

```
udp_recv_channel {
  mcast_join = 239.2.14.22
  port = 8649
  bind = 239.2.14.22
  retry_bind = true
}
udp_recv_channel {
  mcast_join = 239.2.11.71
  port = 8649
  bind = 239.2.11.71
  retry_bind = true
}
```

In this case the IP and port are `239.2.14.22/8649` for the first server and
`239.2.11.71/8649` for the second leading to these startup properties:

```
-Dflume.monitoring.type=gangla
-Dflume.monitoring.hosts=239.2.14.22:8649,239.2.11.71:8649
```

Here, I'm using defaults for poll interval and using the newer ganglia wire protocol.

> While receiving data via TCP is supported in Ganglia, the current
> Flume/Ganglia integration only supports sending data using a multicast
> UDP. If you have a large/complicated network setup, you'll want to get
> educated by your network engineers if things don't work as you expect.

The internal HTTP server

You can configure the Flume agent to start an HTTP server that will output
JSON that can be used by queries using outside mechanisms. Unlike the Ganglia
integration, some external entity has to call into the Flume agent to poll the data.
In theory, you could use Nagios to poll this JSON data and alert on certain conditions,
but I have personally never tried it. Of course this setup is very useful in development
and testing, especially if you are writing custom Flume components to be sure they
are generating useful metrics. Here is a summary of the Java properties you'll need
to set at startup of the Flume agent:

Java property	Value	Description
`flume.monitoring.type`	`http`	Set to `http`
`flume.monitoring.port`	The port number	The port number to bind the HTTP server

The URL for metrics will be as follows:

```
http://SERVER_OR_IP_OF_AGENT:PORT/metrics
```

This is used for the following Flume configuration:

```
agent.sources = s1
agent.channels = c1
gent.sinks = k1
agent.sources.s1.type=avro
agent.sources.s1.bind=0.0.0.0
agent.sources.s1.port=12345
agent.sources.s1.channels=c1
agent.channels.c1.type=memory
agent.sinks.k1.type=avro
agent.sinks.k1.hostname=192.168.33.33
agent.sinks.k1.port=9999
agent.sinks.k1.channel=c1
```

Also, the following startup parameters:

```
-Dflume.monitoring.type=http
-Dflume.monitoring.port=44444
```

Going to `http://SERVER_OR_IP:44444/metrics`, you might see something like the following:

```
{
  "SOURCE.s1":{
    "OpenConnectionCount":"0",
    "AppendBatchAcceptedCount":"0",
    "AppendBatchReceivedCount":"0",
    "Type":"SOURCE",
    "EventAcceptedCount":"0",
    "AppendReceivedCount":"0",
    "StopTime":"0",
    "EventReceivedCount":"0",
    "StartTime":"1365128622891",
    "AppendAcceptedCount":"0"},
  "CHANNEL.c1":{
    "EventPutSuccessCount":"0",
    "ChannelFillPercentage":"0.0",
    "Type":"CHANNEL",
    "StopTime":"0",
    "EventPutAttemptCount":"0",
    "ChannelSize":"0",
    "StartTime":"1365128621890",
    "EventTakeSuccessCount":"0",
    "ChannelCapacity":"100",
    "EventTakeAttemptCount":"0"},
  "SINK.k1":{
    "BatchCompleteCount":"0",
    "ConnectionFailedCount":"4",
    "EventDrainAttemptCount":"0",
    "ConnectionCreatedCount":"0",
    "BatchEmptyCount":"0",
    "Type":"SINK",
    "ConnectionClosedCount":"0",
    "EventDrainSuccessCount":"0",
    "StopTime":"0",
    "StartTime":"1365128622325",
    "BatchUnderflowCount":"0"}
}
```

As you can see, each source, sink, and channel is broken out separately with its corresponding metrics. Each type of source, channel, and sink provides its own set of metric keys, although there is some commonality, so be sure to check what looks interesting. For instance, this Avro Source has OpenConnectionCount, which that is the number of clients connected (and most likely sending data in). This may help you decide if you have the expected number of clients relying on data, or perhaps too many clients and you need to start tiering your agents.

Generally speaking, the channel's ChannelSize or ChannelFillPercentage will give you a good idea of whether data is coming in faster than it is going out. It will also tell you if you have it set large enough for the maintenance/outages for your data volume.

Looking at the sink, EventDrainSuccessCount versus EventDrainAttemptCount will tell you how often output is successful when compared with the times tried. In this example, I configured an Avro Sink to a nonexistent target. As you can see the ConnectionFailedCount value is growing, which is a good indicator of persistent connection problems. Even a growing ConnectionCreatedCount can indicate that connections are dropping and reopening too often.

Really, there are no hard and fast rules besides watching ChannelSize/ChannelFillPercentage. Each use case will have its own performance profile so start small, set up your monitoring, and learn as you go.

Custom monitoring hooks

If you already have a monitoring system, you may want to make the extra effort of developing a custom monitoring reporting mechanism. You may think of it to be as simple as implementing the org.apache.flume.instrumentation. MonitorService interface. You do need to do this, but looking at the interface, you will only see a start() method and a stop() method. Unlike the more obvious Interceptor paradigm, the agent expects that your MonitorService implementation will start/stop a thread to send data on the expected or configured interval if it is the type to send data to a receiving service. If you are going to operate a service, such as the HTTP service, then start/stop would be used to start and stop your listening service. The metrics themselves are published internally to JMX by the various source, sinks, channels, and Interceptors using object names that start with org.apache.flume. Your implementation will need to read these from MBeanServer. The best advice I can give you, should you decide to implement your own, is to look at the source of two existing implementations and do what they do. To use your monitoring hook, set the flume.monitoring.type property to the FQDN of your implementation class. Expect to have to rework any custom hooks with new Flume versions until the framework matures and stabilized.

Summary

In this chapter we covered monitoring Flume agents both from the process level and the monitoring of internal metrics (is it doing work?).

Monit and Nagios were introduced as open source options for process watching.

Next we covered the Flume agent internal monitoring metrics with Ganglia and JSON over HTTP implementations that ship with Apache Flume.

Finally, we covered how to integrate a custom monitoring implementation in case you need to directly integrate directly to some other tool not supported by Flume by default.

In our last chapter we will discuss some general considerations for your Flume deployment.

8

There Is No Spoon – The Realities of Real-time Distributed Data Collection

In this last chapter, I thought we'd cover some of the less concrete, more random thoughts I have around data collection into Hadoop. There's no hard science behind some of this and you should feel perfectly at ease to disagree with me.

While Hadoop is a great tool for consuming vast quantities of data, I often think of a picture of the logjam that occurred in 1886 on the St. Croix River in Minnesota (http://www.nps.gov/sacn/historyculture/stories.htm). When dealing with too much data you want to make sure you don't jam your river. Be sure you take the previous chapter on monitoring seriously and not just as a nice to have.

Transport time versus log time

I had a situation where data was being placed using date patterns in the filename and/or paths in HDFS didn't match the contents of the directories. The expectation was that data in 2013/03/29 contained all the data for March 29, 2013. But the reality was that the date was being pulled from the transport. It turns out that the version of syslog we were using was rewriting the header, including the date portion, causing the data to take on the transport time and not reflect the original time of the record. Usually the offsets were tiny—just a second or two—so nobody really took notice. But then one day one of the relay servers died and when the data, which had got stuck on upstream servers, was finally sent it had the current time. In this case it was shifted by a couple of days. What a mess.

Be sure this isn't happening to you if you are placing data by date. Check the date edge cases to see that they are what you expect, and make sure you test your outage scenarios *before* they happen for real in production.

As I mentioned before, these retransmits due to planned or unplanned maintenance (or even a tiny network hiccup) will most likely cause duplicate and out-of-order events to arrive, so be sure to account for this when processing raw data. There are no single delivery/ordering guarantees in Flume. If you need that, use a transactional database instead.

Time zones are evil

In case you missed my bias against using local time in *Chapter 4, Sinks and Sink Processors*, I'll repeat it here a little stronger—time zones are evil. Evil like Dr. Evil (`http://en.wikipedia.org/wiki/Dr._Evil`)—and let's not forget about its "Mini Me" (`http://en.wikipedia.org/wiki/Mini-Me`) counterpart—daylight savings time.

We live in a global world now. You are pulling data from all over the place into your Hadoop cluster. You may even have multiple data centers in different parts of the country (or the world). The last thing you want to be doing while trying to analyze your data is to deal with askew data. Daylight savings time changes at least somewhere on Earth a dozen times in a year. Just look at the history (`ftp://ftp.iana.org/tz/releases/`). Save yourself a headache and just normalize it to UTC. If you want to convert it to "local time" on its way to human eyeballs, feel free. But while it lives in your cluster, keep it normalized to UTC. Consider adopting UTC everywhere via this Java startup parameter (if you can't set it system-wide):

```
-Duser.timezone=UTC
```

I live in Chicago and our computers at work use Central Time, which adjust for daylight savings. In our Hadoop cluster we like to keep data in a YYYY/MM/DD/HH layout. Twice a year some things break slightly. In the fall, we have twice as much data in our 2 a.m. directory. In the spring there is no 2 a.m. directory. Madness!

Capacity planning

Regardless how much data you think you have, things will change over time. New projects will pop up and data creation rates for your existing projects will change (up or down). Data volume will usually ebb and flow with the traffic of the day. Finally, the number of servers feeding your Hadoop cluster will change over time.

There are many schools of thought on how much extra storage capacity to keep in your Hadoop cluster (we use the totally unscientific value of 20 percent—meaning we usually plan for 80 percent full when ordering additional hardware but don't start to panic until we hit the 85 percent to 90 percent utilization number).

You may also need to set up multiple flows inside a single agent. The source and sink processors are currently single threaded so there is a limit to what tuning batch sizes can accomplish when under heavy data volumes.

The number of Flume agents feeding Hadoop, should be adjusted based on real numbers. Watch the channel size to see how well the writes are keeping up under normal loads. Adjust the maximum channel capacity to handle whatever amount of overhead makes you feel good. You can always spend way more then you need, but even a prolonged outage may overflow the most conservative estimates. This is when you have to pick and choose which data is more important to you and adjust your channel capacities to reflect that. That way, if you exceed your limits, the less important data will be the first to be dropped.

Chances are that your company doesn't have an infinite amount of money and at some point the value of the data versus the cost of continuing to expand your cluster will start to be questioned. This is why setting limits on the volume of data collected is very important. Any project sending data into Hadoop should be able to say what the value of that data is and what the loss is if we delete the older stuff. This is the only way the people writing the checks can make an informed decision.

Considerations for multiple data centers

If you run your business out of multiple data centers and have a large volume of data collected, you may want to consider setting up a Hadoop cluster in each data center rather than sending all your collected data back to a single data center. This will make analyzing the data more difficult as you can't just run one MapReduce job against all the data. Instead you would have to run parallel jobs and then combine the results in a second pass. You can do this with searching and counting problems, but not things such as averages—an average of averages isn't the same as an average.

Pulling all your data into a single cluster may also be more than your networking can handle. Depending on how your data centers are connected to each other, you simply may not be able to transmit your desired volume of data. Finally, consider that a complete cluster failure or corruption may wipe out everything since most clusters are usually too big to back up everything except high value data. Having some of the old data in this case is sometimes better than having nothing. With multiple Hadoop clusters, you have the ability to use a failover sink processor to forward data to a different cluster if you don't want to wait to send to the local one.

If you do choose to send all your data to a single destination, consider adding a large disk capacity machine as a relay server for the data center. This way if there is a communication issue or extended cluster maintenance, you can let data pile up on a machine different than the ones trying to service your customers. This is sound advice even in a single data center situation.

Compliance and data expiry

Remember that the data your company is collecting on your customers may contain sensitive information. You may be bound by other regulatory limitations on access to data such as **Payment Card Industry (PCI**—`http://en.wikipedia.org/wiki/PCI_DSS`) or **Sarbanes Oxley (SOX**—`http://en.wikipedia.org/wiki/Sarbanes%E2%80%93Oxley_Act`). If you aren't properly handling access to this data in your cluster, the government will lean on you or worse, you won't have customers anymore if they feel you aren't protecting their rights and identities. Consider scrambling, trimming, or obfuscating your data of personal information. Chances are the business insight you are looking for falls more into the category of "how many people who search for hammer actually buy one?" rather than "how many customers are named Bob?" As you saw in *Chapter 6, Interceptors*, it would be very easy to write an Interceptor to obfuscate **Personally Identifiable Information (PII**—`http://en.wikipedia.org/wiki/Personally_identifiable_information`) as you move it around.

Your company probably has a document retention policy that most likely includes the data you are putting into Hadoop. Make sure you remove data that your policy says you aren't supposed to be keeping around anymore. The last thing you want is a visit from the lawyers.

Summary

In this chapter we covered several real-world considerations you need to think about when planning your Flume implementation, including the following:

- Transport time not always matching event time
- The mayhem introduced with daylight savings time to your time-based logic
- Capacity planning considerations
- Items to consider when you have more than one data center
- Data compliance
- Data expiration

I hope you enjoyed this book. Hopefully you will be able to apply much of this information directly in your application/Hadoop integration efforts.

Thanks. This was fun.

Index

flume.client.log4j.logger.other 73
flume.client.log4j.log.level 73
flume.client.log4j.message.encoding 73
flume.client.log4j.timestamp 73
Flume headers 73
load balancing 74
properties 73
logStdErr property 50
log time
versus transport time 85, 86

M

MapR
URL 17
MaxBackoff property 74
maxBufferLineLength property 52
maxFileSize, configuration parameter 28
memory-backed channel 25
Memory Channel
about 18, 26
byteCapacityBufferPercentage, configuration parameter 26
byteCapacity, configuration parameter 26
capacity, configuration parameter 26
configuration parameters 26
keep-alive, configuration parameter 26
transactionCapacity, configuration parameter 26
type, configuration parameter 26
minimumRequiredSpace, configuration parameter 28
Monit
about 77, 78
URL 77
multiple data centers
considerations 87
multiplexing channel selector 58
multiport syslog TCP source
about 56
batchSize property 57
channels property 56
charset.default property 57
charset.port.PORT# property 57
eventSize property 57
Facility, header key 57

flume.syslog.status, header key 57
hostname, header key 57
numProcessors property 57
portHeader property 57
ports property 56
priority, header key 57
readBufferSize property 57
timestamp, header key 57
type property 56

N

Nagios
about 78
URL 78
Nagios JMX
flume.monitoring.hosts property 79
flume.monitoring.isGanglia3 property 79
flume.monitoring.pollInterval property 79
flume.monitoring.type property 79
URL 78
name 17
netcat 22
non-durable channel 25
numProcessors property 57

O

org.apache.flume.interceptor.Interceptor interface 68
org.apache.flume.sink.AbstractSink class 33
org.apache.flume.source.AbstractSource class 47

P

Payment Card Industry. *See* **PCI**
PCI 88
Personally Identifiable Information. *See* **PII**
PII 88
Portable Operating System Interface. *See* **POSIX**
portHeader property 57
port parameter 55
port property 54
ports property 56
POSIX 9

Thank you for buying
Apache Flume: Distributed Log Collection for Hadoop

About Packt Publishing

Packt, pronounced 'packed', published its first book "*Mastering phpMyAdmin for Effective MySQL Management*" in April 2004 and subsequently continued to specialize in publishing highly focused books on specific technologies and solutions.

Our books and publications share the experiences of your fellow IT professionals in adapting and customizing today's systems, applications, and frameworks. Our solution based books give you the knowledge and power to customize the software and technologies you're using to get the job done. Packt books are more specific and less general than the IT books you have seen in the past. Our unique business model allows us to bring you more focused information, giving you more of what you need to know, and less of what you don't.

Packt is a modern, yet unique publishing company, which focuses on producing quality, cutting-edge books for communities of developers, administrators, and newbies alike. For more information, please visit our website: www.packtpub.com.

About Packt Open Source

In 2010, Packt launched two new brands, Packt Open Source and Packt Enterprise, in order to continue its focus on specialization. This book is part of the Packt Open Source brand, home to books published on software built around Open Source licences, and offering information to anybody from advanced developers to budding web designers. The Open Source brand also runs Packt's Open Source Royalty Scheme, by which Packt gives a royalty to each Open Source project about whose software a book is sold.

Writing for Packt

We welcome all inquiries from people who are interested in authoring. Book proposals should be sent to author@packtpub.com. If your book idea is still at an early stage and you would like to discuss it first before writing a formal book proposal, contact us; one of our commissioning editors will get in touch with you.

We're not just looking for published authors; if you have strong technical skills but no writing experience, our experienced editors can help you develop a writing career, or simply get some additional reward for your expertise.

Hadoop Beginner's Guide

ISBN: 978-1-84951-730-0   Paperback: 398 pages

Learn how to crunch big data to extract meaning from the data avalanche

1. Learn tools and techniques that let you approach big data with relish and not fear

2. Shows how to build a complete infrastructure to handle your needs as your data grows

3. Hands-on examples in each chapter give the big picture while also giving direct experience

Hadoop Real-World Solutions Cookbook

ISBN: 978-1-84951-912-0   Paperback: 316 pages

Realistic, simple code examples to solve problems at scale with Hadoop and related technologies

1. Solutions to common problems when working in the Hadoop environment

2. Recipes for (un)loading data, analytics, and troubleshooting

3. In depth code examples demonstrating various analytic models, analytic solutions, and common best practices

Please check **www.PacktPub.com** for information on our titles

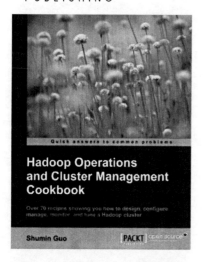

Hadoop Operations and Cluster Management Cookbook

ISBN: 978-1-78216-516-3   Paperback: 350 pages

Over 70 recipes showing you how to design, configure, manage, monitor, and tune a Hadoop cluster

1. Hands-on recipes to configure a Hadoop cluster from bare metal hardware nodes

2. Practical and in depth explanation of cluster management commands

3. Easy-to-understand recipes for securing and monitoring a Hadoop cluster, and design considerations

HBase Administration Cookbook

ISBN: 978-1-84951-714-0   Paperback: 332 pages

Master HBase configuration and administration for optimum database performance

1. Move large amounts of data into HBase and learn how to manage it efficiently

2. Set up HBase on the cloud, get it ready for production, and run it smoothly with high performance

3. Maximize the ability of HBase with the Hadoop eco-system including HDFS, MapReduce, Zookeeper, and Hive

Please check **www.PacktPub.com** for information on our titles

Lightning Source UK Ltd.
Milton Keynes UK
UKOW02f0056281113

221990UK00002B/91/P